T0161990

SIMPLE PRINCIPLES™
TO BECOME A MILLIONAIRE

Alex A. Lluch

Author of Over 3 Million Books Sold!

WS Publishing Group
San Diego, California

SIMPLE PRINCIPLES™
TO BECOME A MILLIONAIRE

By Alex A. Lluch

Published by WS Publishing Group
San Diego, California 92119
Copyright © 2008 by WS Publishing Group

Designed by WS Publishing Group:
David Defenbaugh

For Inquiries:
Logon to www.WSPublishingGroup.com
E-mail info@WSPublishingGroup.com

ISBN 13: 978-1-934386-20-0

Printed in China

Table of Contents

INTRODUCTION

In the land of opportunity, becoming a millionaire is a very realistic achievement. Yet most Americans earn less than $50,000 per year and are saddled with credit-card debt. They have no idea how to save for retirement, let alone how to become a millionaire. But there is no real secret to becoming a millionaire, and anyone, from any background, in any field, with any education level, can do it! Statistics are reassuring when it comes to understanding who can become a millionaire. According to PhDs Thomas J. Stanley and William D. Danko in their book *The Millionaire Next Door*, most millionaires are actually "dull-normal" and self-employed. These folks are "welding contractors, auctioneers, rice farmers, owners of mobile-home parks, pest controllers, coin and stamp dealers, and paving contractors." Admittedly, it will take a lot of work to get from earning an average of $50,000 to your first million but, as Ted Turner has said, making the first million is the most difficult part; after that, the money just keeps on coming in.

What is this book about?

This book is primarily about how to reprogram your mind to believe that you deserve to become wealthy. Financial experts agree that accumulating wealth is 99 percent mindset and 1 percent money. You will discover after reading this book that once you change your thinking it will not be hard to change your financial situation. Changing both your mindset and financial habits will require quite a lot of work; if you are looking for a get-rich-quick scheme, this book is not for you. Keep in mind that hard work and becoming a millionaire go hand in hand, and no one ever got there by taking shortcuts.

Simple Principles™ to Become a Millionaire spends many chapters on your mindset and how it affects your success. If you are not mentally or emotionally capable of receiving wealth, it will remain elusive. To attract wealth, you must create a give and take of energy that functions like a magnet or a boomerang. Think of your thoughts as having a direct connection to the universe. You send out a particular "charge" that either attracts or repels what you desire. Though most of us want the very best in life, we don't actually feel that we deserve it. So, our thoughts and the way we express them come out in such a way that we actually *repel* the very thing we want. This book spends many chapters trying to teach you how to stop *repelling* success and to start *attracting* it.

This book is also about how to take practical steps to identify your goals, create a plan, take action, learn to make good decisions, save money, invest your money, and set up retirement accounts. Reading this book will give you a leg-up on how to consider the whole picture when it comes to your financial vision for your future. This book, in essence, is about turning goals into reality by providing well-researched tips for action.

In fact, the following chapters can be incorporated for success in all areas of your life, including relationships, career management, personal growth, and increasing your overall sense of well-being. The wide appeal of this book is credited to its commitment to lasting results.

Who should read this book?

Simple Principles™ to Become a Millionaire is for everyone who wants to become wealthy. It is for those who are tired of always being broke and living from paycheck to paycheck. It is for people who want to feel secure in their golden years and for those who want to plan for the future of their family. The information in this book can be applied to anyone who is ready to make a change in their mindset and who wants to accumulate wealth. This book will benefit just about anyone, including college students, professionals who want to earn more money, and those who are ready to start to plan for their retirement.

This book is for people who want to:

- Increase their income
- Realize that they deserve wealth
- Earn more than they spend
- Feel in control of their finances
- Reduce the amount of credit-card debt in their lives
- Reduce financial uncertainty

- Increase savings
- Improve their ability to influence others
- Sell their ideas
- Communicate more effectively
- Set and achieve goals
- Feel comfortable taking responsible risks
- Learn to develop patience
- Create an effective network
- Learn to think like a millionaire
- Learn more about investing
- Increase their willpower
- Make better decisions
- Turn inaction into action
- Create a viable wealth strategy

Even if you already happen to be a millionaire, reading the 200 tips, tricks, suggestions, and pieces of advice and wisdom contained in this book will be solid reinforcement to the strategies you already practice. The chapters on positive thinking are sure to benefit people in any income bracket. Thus, this inspirational book will surely come in handy at just about any time in your life that you need a quick tip on how to streamline your efforts toward success.

Why should you read this book?

Picking up this book indicates you already have the desire to become a millionaire. What holds many of us back, however, is a lack of knowledge, discipline, and commitment to our goals. Here are some questions to ask yourself if you are wondering whether this book is right for you:

- Are you tired of being broke?
- Are creditors calling your home or job?
- Are you comfortable taking risks?
- Are you an emotional spender?
- Do you spend more money than you earn?
- Do you want to purchase a home of your own?
- Do you think, "I will never be rich"?
- Do you know how to control your imagination?
- Do you have difficulty waiting for results?
- Do you want to learn how to invest your money?
- Do you want to understand available retirement accounts?
- Are you ready to change your financial future?
- Are you tired of living paycheck to paycheck?

These are just a few of the more than 200 topics covered in this book. Nearly everyone, at some point, has been able to identify with one or more of the above questions. If this applies to you, then read on. Rest assured that the principles in this book are well-researched and can be applied by virtually anyone who is ready for change. Its compact size makes it easy to keep with you for quick reference. This book will empower you to make life-altering decisions for a secure financial future. Finally, you should read this book because you are finally ready to admit that you do, in fact, have control over your own life!

WHAT IT MEANS TO BE
A MILLIONAIRE

When you consider that 70 percent of Americans live from paycheck to paycheck and that 62 percent of Americans do not regularly contribute to a savings account, becoming a millionaire can mean the difference between barely getting by and living a comfortable lifestyle. Learning the skills it requires to become a millionaire incorporates discipline and the ability to delay instant gratification. These are skills that are beneficial for all aspects of life—but particularly when it comes to spending. Becoming a millionaire means learning to control spending and to always bring in more than you spend. This mindset is in direct contradiction to how most of us live. A recent survey found that the average American spends $1.22 for every $1 he earns. This chronic overspending has catastrophic effects for one hoping to have financial security. Thus, becoming a millionaire means having the desire to change how you think about money and then the willpower to stick to some basic financial principles—with 100 percent commitment.

Who Can Become a Millionaire?

It would be nice to say that anyone can become a millionaire, but the fact is only those who are willing to effect real change in their lives and take major action toward their goals are going to make it. So, if you are ready to shift your priorities from instant gratification toward achievement of long-term goals then you will be able to become a millionaire.

One very important consideration for becoming a millionaire is your education level. Consider that 80 percent of millionaires have a college or advanced degree. (However, keep in mind, education is not absolutely necessary for becoming a millionaire; multimillionaire Michael Dell, owner of Dell Computer Corporation, is a college dropout.) There are several ways to get a degree in this day and age, including online programs for those who have full-time work and/or family commitments. It is also necessary to realize that working 35 hours per week will not bring you the financial windfall you desire. To bring in that extra cash, you're going to have to up the ante and put in some overtime. A recent survey found that 66 percent of millionaires work between 45 and 55 hours per week and many admitted working extra hours from home after having left the office.

The best and fastest way to accumulate wealth is to stop racking up debt. Consider the following statistics: 185 million Americans have at least one credit card, though the average number of cards per household is 6.5. The average household owes $8,562 in credit-card debt, and 95 percent of car owners finance one or more autos at an average of $375 per month for 60 months. At this rate, it is no wonder there are so few millionaires in America! By taking steps now to reduce debt and increase your income, you can position yourself to make other financial decisions that will lead you to reaching your goal of becoming a millionaire.

Recognize that Wealth Is More than Money

It is great to want something badly enough that you are relentless in its achievement. Indeed, having the courage and discipline to do what is necessary to achieve your goals can be very rewarding. This cycle can lead to prosperity, happiness, and the attainment of great knowledge. However, it should always be balanced with the other aspects of your life. Becoming a millionaire is without a doubt going to take up much of your time and energy. It is true that you are going to have to work from the inside out—first to change your thought patterns and then to reflect those changes in your financial decisions.

Several times throughout this process make sure to step back and evaluate your wealth at this moment. When adding up your net worth, be sure to add in your family, friends, achievements, travels, and memories with your funds. Doing so often will remind you of all that you currently have and prevent you from becoming so obsessed with increasing your wealth that you forget about what really matters in life: your relationships. Keep in mind that the majority of Americans— 55 percent across all income brackets—report that they are always worried about money and that 95 percent of couples admit that they argue regularly about finances. Indeed, it is true that money will not solve all of your problems. It is a good idea, therefore, to get your life in order while trying to accumulate wealth so that you do not depend on money to fix what may be broken in other departments.

With Wealth Comes Great Responsibility

Remember that in the end you cannot take your money with you. So, while you should plan to take care of your family, dependents, and friends after your passing, it is also the responsibility of the wealthy to give something back to the universe that blessed them with abundance. Take inspiration from the rags-to-riches story of philanthropist and author J.K. Rowling. Rowling, who authored the 7 wildly successful *Harry Potter* books, was once living out of her car and penniless. Rowling, however, never gave up her dream of penning the now-famous series. She currently finds herself 1 among just 35 of the elite *Forbes* list of female *billionaires.* Rowling exhibits gratitude and gives back by contributing a substantial amount of money to charities that combat poverty and social inequality. She also donates to multiple sclerosis research and to organizations that aid one-parent families. Rowling wisely said, "I think you have a moral responsibility when you've been given far more than you need to do wise things with it and give intelligently."

Keep in mind that you can give back to your community from any income level. In fact, if you begin your charitable pursuits now, you will find it easier to allow them to grow with your income. Assimilating giving into your current lifestyle taps into the give-and-take nature of how the universe operates and will most assuredly put you on the receiving end of abundance. Know that there is no time like the present to begin giving back. If you are curious about various charitable organizations, visit www.charitynavigator.org to find out more.

Maximizing the Benefits of This Book

Congratulations! By deciding to read this book you are taking your first step toward long-term financial independence. Keep in mind that it is not enough to simply read this book. You must take what you've learned and apply it. Pay particular attention to areas in which you need the most improvement. For example, if you are chronically indecisive, spend extra time in the "Making the Right Decisions" chapter. If you find it hard to believe that you will ever be wealthy, "Believing in Yourself" might be the chapter that speaks loudest to you.

Finally, always keep this book handy. Put it in the glove box of your car. Stick it in the top drawer of your desk at work. Lay it on your nightstand before bed. Pull it from your briefcase or purse while waiting for appointments. Keep it in your gym bag. This book is written to be read over and over again. The principles will take time to sink in, so the idea is to read this book and practice the contents often. Remember that becoming a millionaire is a long-term goal that will take time, patience, and discipline.

PREPARING FOR WEALTH

The best way to prepare yourself for wealth is by adopting a multidisciplinary perspective. In other words, you must prepare yourself on 3 different levels for wealth: mentally, emotionally, and financially. To start, you must open your mind to seeing yourself as a wealthy person; gain control over emotions that prevent you from becoming wealthy; and make realistic changes regarding how you manage your finances. Know that above all, the path to wealth begins with your mind. Financial experts agree that unless you are ready to receive wealth, it will always be just out of reach.

One of the first ways to prepare your mind for wealth is to release any guilt associated with its accumulation. As long as you intend to engage in ethical practices, there is no reason to feel guilty about being rich. Billionaire Oprah Winfrey once said in an interview with *People* magazine, "I was coming back from Africa on one of my trips. I had taken one of my wealthy friends with me. She said, 'Don't you just feel guilty? Don't you just feel terrible?' I said, 'No, I don't. I do not know how me being destitute is going to help them.' Then I said when we got home, 'I'm going home to sleep on my Pratesi sheets right now and I'll feel good about it.'" Oprah had gone on this particular trip to Africa to scout locations for the girls' academy she built in South Africa. Her story reminds us that it is critical to feel worthy of what you have and, at the same time, be willing to share it.

The next major mental challenge to overcome is to be sure you are open to receiving wealth. The way to open your wealth receptors is to focus on what you already have. Do this by expressing gratitude each morning and night. List the people and things in your life that currently make up your fortune. Truly appreciating and focusing on them will ultimately attract more wealth. With this in mind, read the following simple principles on preparing yourself for wealth. They offer several practical suggestions for preparing your mind and spirit for the great wealth that can soon be yours.

Principle #1

Learn to manage your money.

— ❋ —

Managing your money is more than just casual budgeting; it is accounting for how every cent you earn is spent. This includes establishing a strict budget for expenses, paying down debt, and saving. No matter how much money you earn, it is important to manage it — for if you fail to manage what you currently have, you will fail to be responsible for more of it. Interestingly, studies show that 80 percent of lottery winners file for bankruptcy within 5 years of cashing in their ticket. This happens because they do not have the skills required to handle so much cash. Make sure you do by learning money-management skills today.

Principle #2

Order the least expensive thing on a pricey menu.

Putting yourself in wealthy environments is one of the best ways to prepare yourself for wealth. Indeed, more important than what you actually order is the experience of feeling wealthy. So get dressed up and dine at the most expensive restaurant in town. Read the menu carefully and savor the choices. Ask your server questions about the specials and peruse the wine list. Absorb every bit of the experience by inhaling deeply and making eye contact with other wealthy patrons. When you are ready, order the least expensive thing on the menu and say you're fine with "just water." This way, you can learn to have a high-brow dining experience at a fraction of the cost.

Principle #3

Never buy fakes.

Developing a millionaire mindset is primarily about feeling worthy of great wealth. In order for this mental transformation to take hold, it must be genuine and thorough. This must extend to purchases that you make, too. Therefore, if you decide you want a Rolex watch or a Fendi handbag, save up until you have enough money to buy the real thing. Buying fakes reinforces the message that you are not deserving of the real thing. The truth is quite the contrary! Remind yourself that you are better off owning a real Timex than a fake Rolex.

Principle #4

Tip well.

Tipping well is a great way to feel like a big spender without actually being one. According to *American Demographic* magazine, not surprisingly, the poorer a person is, the more likely he or she will avoid tipping. Those Americans who do tip add about 17 percent onto the bill. If you round that just a few points, you can be seen as a big spender while only adding a few dollars to the total. Be sure to tip at least 20 percent when you go out for dinner or drinks. Likewise, hand singles out to bag handlers, cab drivers, and delivery people. Tipping well will make you feel rich without actually costing you very much.

PRINCIPLE #5

Buy cheap seats for a rich experience.

Learn to enjoy expensive entertainment inexpensively — it is an important part of preparing for wealth. Great ways to save on high-brow entertainment include buying balcony seats at the orchestra, getting tickets to the matinee showing of an event, and purchasing last-minute "day of" tickets to Broadway and off-Broadway productions. Likewise, dress up for a day at the races or a fancy casino, but refrain from betting; visit exclusive stores and try on expensive clothes; or tour a winery and ask to hold the most expensive bottle of wine they sell — and then taste one you can afford.

Principle #6

Remember that charity attracts abundance.

It is true that the more you give, the more you receive. Indeed, for every dollar you donate think of yourself as receiving 10 credits toward abundance. Abundance reveals itself in many ways — both through good karma and feeling the satisfaction that comes from contributing to your community. Additionally, remember your gifts are tax deductible, and the actual cost of the donation is reduced by your tax savings. For example, if you are in the 33 percent tax bracket, the actual cost of a $100 donation is only $67 ($100 less the $33 tax savings). Thus, the more money you donate, the larger the tax break and the more the charity will actually receive.

Principle #7

Learn the true meaning of wealth.

We often forget to include important things when we evaluate our wealth. Wealth is more than money and assets. It is the true collection of people, places, experiences, and opportunities that make us rich individuals. When you calculate your worth, don't forget to include each member of your family and friends. Include valuable life lessons you've learned as well as your most precious memories. List your career accomplishments and other awards. Factor in your education and travel experiences. Once you see the priceless parts that make up the whole of your life you will realize the true meaning of wealth.

Principle #8

Become indispensable at work.

The job market is increasingly unstable. It used to be that high-wage earners were protected from getting a pink slip, but no more. Companies lay off thousands of employees every day. According to a recent survey, a whopping 44 percent of workers who were let go in 2005 earned $85,000 per year or more. To prepare yourself for wealth in these times, it is important to protect yourself by becoming indispensable at your job. Become the go-to guy — the guy who does extra work without being asked, who others look to for answers, who works overtime when necessary. In short, be the guy who your company cannot function without.

Principle #9

Realize that money will not solve all of your problems.

It is unrealistic to think that having a million dollars will solve your problems. It may offer financial relief, but your thoughts, values, outlook, and ethics will stay the same unless you change them. For example, if you and your spouse fight about money, don't assume the fighting will stop when there is more of it. It won't — there will just be more money to fight over. Similarly, if you struggle with depression, becoming a millionaire will only result in you becoming a depressed millionaire. Have realistic expectations about the effect increased wealth will have on you.

THINKING LIKE A MILLIONAIRE

If you are to become a millionaire, you must first think like one. Start by imagining you are financially independent — and don't be afraid to think big! As billionaire Donald Trump once said, "As long as you're going to be thinking anyway, think big." So imagine yourself as a millionaire. Figure out who you will become with the benefits and freedoms being a millionaire affords. Thinking like a millionaire is like trying on an expensive suit — it prepares you for wearing one. By getting used to high-quality fabric and the cut of a suit in advance, you will look comfortable walking around in it the day you need to put it on. Similarly, try on the idea of becoming a millionaire. Do this by exploring your ideas about wealth.

When you consider your perception of being rich, what qualities come to mind? Do you picture greed, mistrust, and back-biting? Or, do you imagine security, luxury, and philanthropy? Shape your thoughts toward the positive, because your mind will not allow you to move forward if you believe the end-result of wealth is unethical or negative. A way to avoid the mind-trap of negative associations with wealth is to invest time researching millionaires whom you admire. People such as Oprah Winfrey, Steve Jobs, Michael Dell, and Bill Gates are all examples of people who admirably obtained their wealth and continue to use it to impressive, even noble, ends. Look to such people for examples of what you would like to do with your money. Learn everything you can about those folks and then imagine yourself living as they do.

If it is impossible for you to imagine yourself wealthy, you have just discovered something critically important: that you are your own biggest obstacle to wealth. You must combat thinking that prevents success. To do this, identify what your thoughts and feelings are regarding money and the people who have it. The following principles will help you do this. They will also direct you toward thinking and feeling like a millionaire. Above all, use the following principles to tap into your greatest source of wealth: your imagination. As Steve Forbes once said, "The real source of wealth and capital in this new era is not material things. ... It is the human mind, the human spirit, the human imagination, and our faith in the future."

Principle #10

Realize that your mind already knows how to become a millionaire.

———————————— ⁕ ————————————

Author Ayn Rand wisely wrote, "Wealth is the product of man's capacity to think." It may seem impossible, but you already know how to become wealthy. However, you have buried this knowledge beneath years of accumulated self-doubt and fear. Chip away at this crust that blocks your successful thoughts by tuning in to your inner-achiever. Let your mind wander to a time before self-doubt and fear took over — to a time when there was endless possibility. Write down whatever comes to mind. This is your first exercise in training yourself to think like a millionaire.

Principle #11

Rewire your financial hard drive.

Your financial hard drive is the stuff and guts on which you base all financial decisions in your life. This hard drive was constructed through the lessons you learned watching adults handle and discuss money when you were growing up. Your brain absorbed this information and used it to create your hard drive, which informs your opinion of what money is and what you are ultimately worth. To increase your wealth, you must rewire your hard drive. This means changing the way you think about money and your self-worth. You can do this by making connections with new, positive thoughts.

PRINCIPLE #12

Develop your millionaire mind.

— ❋ —

What is your financial mindset? Do you think of yourself as poor or middle class? If so, then you will *always* be poor or middle class. Each of us can only be as rich as our minds allow, so start thinking of yourself as a millionaire. Practice thinking rich by imagining what you will do when you reach wealth. Write these dreams down and post them where you will see them often. Repeat "I am a millionaire" over and over several times a day. After a while, your actions will start to reflect your millionaire mindset as you are more frequently drawn to lucrative opportunities.

Principle #13

Change the way you view rich people.

---- ✳ ----

If you view rich people as greedy, selfish, snobby, or untrustworthy, no wonder you are not wealthy! Your mind is protecting you from becoming someone you dislike. Change your mind about what it means to be rich by focusing on rich people you can admire. For instance, Microsoft founder and billionaire Bill Gates started the Bill and Melinda Gates Foundation through which he and his wife donate billions to charity. Focusing on positive images of wealthy people can help your mind lower its defenses and allow you to get on track to joining the millionaire club.

Principle #14

Think long term and keep your eye on the prize.

Studies show that the most successful people have long-term goals that they work toward every single day. They adapt their lifestyles to meet the demands of their dream. If your dream is to become a millionaire, you must always keep that in the forefront of your mind as you make daily decisions. Best-selling author and businessman Brian Tracy says the combination of working toward your long-term goals and not giving in to every impulse to spend your money will get you on your way to financial independence.

PRINCIPLE #15

Know that you deserve to become a millionaire.

What do you think you deserve? Spend some real time with this question, because your entire life will unfold before you, based on your answer. Indeed, if you do not feel worthy of the lifestyle that prosperity affords, then your thoughts will taint your actions and keep you from your goal. If you wish to walk the road of wealth, you must first believe deep down that you deserve to accumulate wealth.

Principle #16

Express your intention to become wealthy to the universe.

Rich people attract more wealth. Why? Because they think, act, and behave wealthy. Rhonda Byrnes, author of the best-selling book *The Secret*, describes this phenomenon as the law of attraction. The theory works like a boomerang. If you spend your energy thinking, "I'll always be broke," then you are sure to get what you asked for. Instead, transform your thoughts into positive, money-making energy by telling the universe that you intend to prosper. This releases your intention to become wealthy to the collective world energy. Do this and you will find all paths lead you in the direction of your dream of becoming a millionaire.

Principle #17

Be motivated by your own drive.

What drives you to become a millionaire? Take the time to hone in on your motivations. This is an important step, because if you are not doing this for yourself, odds are you will not succeed. If your efforts are to show others how successful you are or to exact revenge, you will become distracted and fail. However, if your reasons for becoming a millionaire are grounded in your own personal growth and a part of your individual mission statement, your chance for success increases tenfold.

Principle #18

Change your emotional response to money.

Your thoughts and behaviors regarding money are directed by how you feel about it. For instance, you may think that once you "make it" you won't have time to enjoy the spoils of your efforts, and then what's the point? Thinking this way makes you feel hopeless and prevents you from taking steps toward wealth. Instead, focus on things that make you feel good about accumulating wealth, like living in a comfortable house, putting your kids through college, traveling, or being in a position to make large donations to your favorite charity.

PRINCIPLE #19

Realize that your comfort zone is holding you back—then step outside of it.

The fact is that people who are comfortable do not grow. This is because remaining in a comfort zone encourages a person to do the bare minimum — their only goal is to keep things the same way they've always been. To become a millionaire you must push yourself outside of your safety zone over and over again. Pushing your limits is like stretching your body. You will know it's working when you start to feel uncomfortable. When you feel that twinge, be assured that you are inching your way closer to your ultimate goal of being a millionaire.

BELIEVING IN YOURSELF

It seems obvious that in order to be successful, you must believe in yourself. Yet, most of us have been trained to focus on the things we can't do rather than on what we can. Studies repeatedly show that changing your focus to a "can-do" attitude will dramatically increase your confidence. In fact, a 2001 study published in the *Journal of Counseling Psychology* found that people who had hip and knee replacement or reconstructive surgery recovered faster when they believed in their ability to do what was required for their recovery. The study reported, "Those with more confidence in their ability to achieve their goals tended to be more successful in rehabilitation than those with weaker beliefs in their own ability to make a positive difference." Furthermore, thinking positively about your pursuits and abilities also encourages you to trust that you can do whatever it is you set your mind to—including becoming a millionaire.

The fact is that on the road to wealth there are no limits except for the ones you put upon yourself. So take a look at how you perceive your abilities. Start by analyzing your responses to the tasks required to achieve your goals. When you think about the steps you must take to increase your wealth, do you become overwhelmed? Are you tempted to give up? Do you think, "I will never be a millionaire — what's the point in trying?" If so, tear down these negative ruts of thinking and replace them with kind and loving thoughts about yourself. As the British writer Samuel Johnson once noted, "Self-confidence is the first requisite to great undertakings." The following principles will help you realize that continuing to focus on what you cannot do will not bring you any closer to your goals. Use them to guide you to a place in which you feel comfortable believing in your ability to become a millionaire.

Principle #20

Believe you will be rich, and you will be rich.

— ❋ —

Every single millionaire has stated at some point that they were not able to be open to the opportunities that were presented to them until they believed they deserved them. It is clear that in order to succeed you must believe that you will reach your goals. How else to stay motivated and on track? C. S. Lewis wisely wrote, "We are what we believe we are." So, start believing that you are rich. Beginning with your mind will allow action to follow.

Principle #21

Become a role model.

People who are role models report feeling inspired to work harder. Because someone is depending on them for inspiration, they must articulate and achieve important goals. Role models also tend to live life to its fullest in order to show the person they mentor how to succeed. This active approach to living will show others that you can be counted on to achieve goals. So become a role model or mentor to a child, student, coworker, or family member. You will boost your self-esteem, allowing you to accomplish anything you set your mind on.

PRINCIPLE #22

Count yourself among the experts you admire.

Expert knowledge about how to become a millionaire is available to you at any time. To put yourself on par with other millionaires, start reading everything you can that is written by or about them. Some of the most successful people in the world have written dozens of articles and books on how they became wealthy. Study their experiences, decisions, and philosophies to follow in their footsteps. After you have done this, you can count yourself among the experts you admire! Knowledge will give you confidence that you can achieve what others before you have done.

Principle #23

Don't be afraid of failure.

Millionaires know to expect that at times, you will encounter failure on the path to wealth. The founder of Honda Motor Company, Soichiro Honda, once said, "Success is 99 percent failure." Indeed, part of learning what works is also learning what doesn't. Instead of beating yourself up for the things at which you might occasionally fail, realize they are small steps on the path toward larger successes. Never waste time lamenting failure instead of learning the lessons imbedded in each experience. Making room for failure is an indispensable tool to learn as you become a wealthier person.

Principle #24

Turn your mistakes into experience.

No one enjoys making mistakes, but as Albert Einstein once said, "Anyone who has never made a mistake has never tried anything new." The fact is, you are going to make mistakes while forging your path to wealth. It may be difficult at first, but you must learn to view mistakes as experience points you accumulate on your life's journey. As you learn from your mistakes, remember that your greatest ally is your belief that you will succeed. At every turn, prevent self-doubt from creeping in when you err.

PRINCIPLE #25

Remind yourself that your beliefs are not set in stone.

Your belief system is formed over years through reinforcement. For this reason, the older we get, the more entrenched in our beliefs we become. However, it is not impossible to change your beliefs. You should especially work to change the ones that work against your ability to become a millionaire. Many of us spend countless hours focusing on what we cannot do rather than on what we can. Over time, this leads to a sense of futility and a lack of faith in our ability to reach our goals. Start believing in yourself today by replacing all "I can't" thoughts with "I can."

Principle #26

Get back in the saddle.

We've all heard that if we fall off a horse, it is best to immediately get back in the saddle so fear does not have time to overtake us. This is true in all aspects of life, and especially of becoming a millionaire. Be prepared for a few falls here and there, and never let yourself be crippled by short-term failures. No one became a millionaire by giving up at the first setback, and neither will you. As you become better at rebounding after a fall, your self-confidence will strengthen, preparing you to handle anything thrown at you on the path to becoming a millionaire.

Principle #27

Don't give up, live up.

No matter what happens on the road to becoming a millionaire, never ever give up. In fact, when you sit down to write out your goals, put "don't give up" high on the list. If at any point on your journey you feel yourself losing confidence in your ability to become a millionaire, chant to yourself, "Don't give up, live up!" To live up means to always pursue your goals and follow your dreams. Repeat this mantra over and over until you feel that the urge to quit has passed. You should even record yourself saying this message and play it while you sleep during especially difficult times.

Principle #28

Trust your instincts.

Many of us look outside of ourselves for guidance on important decisions. This is because we do not trust our own judgment. Living this way will deplete your personal power over time and make it impossible to succeed. As Ralph Waldo Emerson wisely wrote, "Self-trust is the first secret of success." To become a millionaire you must learn to trust your instincts. You can develop confidence in your instincts by testing them in a series of smaller decisions. By exercising your instincts on smaller matters, they will become practiced for bigger decisions.

Principle #29

Experience pride by expressing hidden talents.

Learn to believe in yourself by encouraging talents you've let fall by the wayside. For example, if you like to write but rarely make time for it, sit down and start writing something every day — perhaps join a writer's group to get you motivated. If you used to play an instrument, dig it out of the garage and pick it up again. You may be creaky at first, but, much like riding a bike, your hidden talents will come back to you with time. Share what you've written with people who will appreciate it, and make sure to admire your own work. Focusing on and developing your talents has an immediate positive effect on your sense of confidence.

PRINCIPLE #30

Never compare your wealth to others.

———————————— ✳ ————————————

While it is tempting to look to others to gauge your performance, your best measuring stick is, in fact, yourself. Focus on recognizing your own strengths, weaknesses, and abilities to realistically judge your own wealth. The truth of the matter is that someone, somewhere will earn more or invest better than you. If you fixate on beating others or being beaten, you'll never give yourself a chance to celebrate when you have accomplished something truly incredible in your own right. Don't let the brightness of someone else's accomplishments cast shadows on your own light.

Principle #31

Recognize that you can learn new skills.

———————— ✳ ————————

Becoming a millionaire may involve learning a new skill set, such as becoming an expert in computer technology or learning how to invest in the stock market. Don't be daunted by the prospect of having to learn a field from the bottom up. Instead, treat it as an opportunity to learn something that will be profitable for the rest of your life. Just because you are not a computer specialist does not mean you cannot learn to build websites. Likewise, just because you are new to the stock market does not mean you can't become an expert investor. Millionaires prove to themselves that they can do it.

Principle #32

Learn to sell yourself.

————————— ✳ —————————

A recent poll of American businesses found that a whopping 76 percent of promotions are given to those who pursue them. That means that just 34 percent of all people are promoted without asking. Never assume your boss knows that you want to be promoted. Make your wants clear. Ask what paths a person in your place of business can take to be promoted. Make sure the right people know about your professional accomplishments. Work with your manager to put together a promotion timetable. Millionaires put themselves on the fast track to success; they don't wait for it to be handed to them.

Principle #33

Recognize that your level of success depends on your opinion of yourself.

If you place a low value on your self-worth, you can be sure your level of success will be substandard. Therefore, it is critical to put a premium on your opinions, ideas, and efforts. For inspiration, look to business mogul Oprah Winfrey, who never for a moment stopped believing in herself. In an interview with the Academy of Achievement, Winfrey stated, "In the fourth grade was when I first, I think, began to believe in myself. For the first time I believed I could do almost anything. I felt I was the queen bee. I felt I could control the world." Winfrey's belief in herself is evident in everything she does and was a key factor in her achievement of wealth.

Using Your Imagination

Incredibly, the imagination is an often-overlooked tool for becoming successful and wealthy. This is because many adults liken using one's imagination to daydreaming or "goofing off." However, nothing could be further from the truth. As Napoleon Hill, author of the groundbreaking book *Think and Grow Rich*, wrote, "Imagination is the workshop of the mind." Indeed, a person's imagination is where all desire, impulse, and creative thought is born. Each of these traits is usually possessed by those people who have become millionaires.

There are two basic types of imagination — automatic and controlled. Automatic imagining occurs when you suddenly feel inspired with a great idea. Another example is when your brain conjures up images as you read or listen to a narrator tell a story. Automatic imagining is an excellent way to brainstorm your way to new inventions, creative solutions, or other out-of-the-box type of ideas. Use automatic imagining to open your mind up to the infinite ways you can think, feel, act like, and become a millionaire. In other words, use your automatic imagination to think beyond your wildest dreams!

Next, harness the power of automatic imagining to master a technique called controlled imagining. Controlled imagining is when you train your brain to associate positive images with your goals. For instance, when you plan for retirement, instead of picturing yourself destitute and in a nursing home, use controlled imagining to picture images of abundance, relaxation, and family. Mastering controlled imagination takes practice. When you find yourself sparked by an inspirational thought or idea, let it unfold naturally. See where it goes and notice whether the images support or negate your aspirations. If they support your goals, refine the image by controlling what you add to it. For example, if you are inspired to start your own business, focus your imagination on images of success — and be specific. Picture yourself with several employees and numerous loyal customers. Take it a step further and picture yourself winning a small business award from your community. If you naturally conjure images that negate your goals, however, use controlled imagining to replace the negative images with positive ones. Practicing controlled imagination is how you will create a mindset and a reality to support your goals.

Use the following simple principles to ignite your imagination. With practice, you can use your imagination as a tool to work with on your journey to wealth.

Principle #34

Realize that imagination is for grown-ups, too.

Imagination is not just for children! Though children are often more comfortable using their imaginations, adults have a tremendous amount to gain by refining theirs. Using your imagination allows you to explore new ideas that can change your life. Allowing yourself to daydream for a few minutes every day will inspire creativity, which is critical for coming up with your game plan for how you will become a millionaire. Another bonus of using your imagination to picture all possible outcomes of a situation is a sharpened set of analytical skills. So use your imagination — it's not just child's play.

Principle #35

Choose imagination over practicality.

———————— ❋ ————————

Sometimes we think in such practical terms, we block our ability to conjure up fantastic ideas. For example, when you go to write down steps to reach your goal of becoming a millionaire, you may find your practical side thinking, "That will never work," or "Such a goal will take too long." Don't ruin your brainstorming process with such thoughts! Instead, let your mind drift beyond the words on the page. Use your imagination to reshape whatever preconceived notions you have about how to reach your goal.

Principle #36

Use imagination to catch great ideas.

———————————— ✳ ————————————

Henry David Thoreau once wrote, "If you have built castles in the air, your work need not be lost; that is where they should be. Now put the foundations under them." In this spirit, allow your dreams to form the basis of your goals. Start by letting yourself daydream. When you feel inspired, write down your ideas, using different interpretations until they take shape. Let's say you imagined yourself standing in the center of a hip, bustling, downtown cafe. Turn this vision into a goal of owning your own restaurant. In this spirit, use your ability to dream to catch great ideas like brilliant butterflies in a net.

Principle #37

Recognize that all creative thought starts with the imagination.

There is no deep secret to creative thinking. Creative people simply know how to use their imagination. The imagination is the root of all creative thought, so learn to use it! If you are stumped by what to do next, employ your imagination to help come up with new ideas. Or practice "stream of consciousness" by writing whatever comes to mind and see what ideas flow to the page. Meditate and see what images are conjured up by your mind's eye. Sing, paint, sketch, or build your way to a new idea, invention, or process. You may be surprised at the novel ideas that surface when you get creative.

PRINCIPLE #38

Imagine that money is flowing into your bank account.

———————— ✳ ————————

Use your imagination to convince yourself that you are already accumulating the wealth you desire. Be specific! Actually visualize a vault in a bank that is filling up with your money. This tool is recommended by most major financial experts. In fact, Napoleon Hill, author of the best-selling book *Think and Grow Rich*, recommended imagining you already have all the money you need and to use repetition of thought to imagine that you "see and feel money in your hands." This type of imagining creates thoughts that point you in the direction of lucrative opportunities, thereby exponentially increasing your chances of becoming a millionaire.

Principle #39

Recognize that imagination is more important than anything else.

— ✳ —

Albert Einstein once said, "Imagination is more important than knowledge. For knowledge is limited, whereas imagination embraces the entire world." Indeed, there is a limit to how much one can learn about a particular field or skill if they fail to use their imagination. Think of your imagination as the booster jet that gets you to the next level, as the magic sneakers that propel you to higher ground. Whether you want to come up with an actual invention or to simply invent a plan of action, be sure to put your imagination to work.

Principle #40

Never use your imagination negatively.

———————————— ✳ ————————————

As adults, we often use our powerful imaginations as weapons rather than tools. We let our imaginations run wild with fear by imagining worst-case scenarios or conjuring up images that irrationally paralyze. To become a millionaire you must avoid wasting your imagination on negative thoughts. Nine times out of 10 those thoughts are completely ridiculous and not based in reality. Worse, such thoughts actually attract negative outcomes. An uncontrolled imagination can cause a person to feel out of control and fearful. As best-selling self-help author Louise Hay has written, "Every thought we think is creating our future." Thus, make sure you use your imagination to create a future you want.

PRINCIPLE #41

Imagine with all of your senses.

When imagining yourself as a millionaire, be sure to engage all your senses. For example, see yourself buying a new home. Picture every detail of the house. Look at the front door and picture yourself stepping across the threshold of your home. Imagine your hand running over the surfaces, touching door knobs and window sills. Take a deep breath and inhale the scent of the wood and fresh paint—the smell of *newness*. Next, listen to the sounds of the floorboards creaking and of the house settling at night. Finally, imagine the taste of the first family meal you will share in your very own home.

Principle #42

Use your imagination to hone other skills.

Rather than being a capricious, wasteful endeavor, using one's imagination can have benefits far beyond daydreaming and mustering up creativity. In fact, using one's imagination has been shown to improve analytical skills and memory. A 2004 study by the National Institute on Aging (NIA) found that using their imagination helps older people remember to take medications and follow other medical advice. Researchers found older adults who spend time picturing how they would test their blood sugar were 50 percent more likely to actually do these tests on a regular basis than those who used other memory techniques.

Principle #43

Use imagination to change your life.

The human imagination is so powerful it can actually be used to change your life. Indeed, it is during the process of imagining that we become able to create the ideas, thoughts, goals, and desires that develop into the backbones of our entire life's purpose. Psychoanalyst Carl Jung was one person who used his imagination to crystallize his life's purpose. He once wrote, "The years when I was pursuing my inner images were the most important in my life. In them, everything essential was decided." Use your imagination to conjure up the ideas, thoughts, goals, and desires that will become the cornerstones of your wealthy life.

Affirmations and Visualizations

Amazingly, humans have the ability to create our own reality just by using our thoughts. And yet, for most of us, more than 50 percent of our thoughts each day are negative. According to the National Science Foundation, most people think an average of 1,000 thoughts per hour. Deep thinkers are found to think twice as many thoughts per hour, or as many as 50,000 thoughts per day—and 25,000 of these thoughts each day are negative and discouraging! This means an overwhelming majority of your brainpower is being used to prevent success rather than to facilitate it.

To become a millionaire, you must create your own reality using your thoughts — and doing this will require changing the way you use your brain. You can change your brain using powerful mental techniques known as affirmations and visualizations. Indeed, leading financial experts, such as Napoleon Hill, T. Harv Eker, Anthony Robbins, and Brian Tracy, insist that using affirmations and visualizations is necessary to developing a millionaire mindset.

Affirmations are messages you repeatedly tell yourself, such as "I will succeed," "I am a smart and interesting person," or "I can accomplish this goal." Over time, affirmations teach your brain to accept these messages as the truth. The repetitive quality of affirmations functions like an exercise; your brain is improved from having positive messages drilled into it in the same way your biceps are improved from doing reps on a weight machine.

The second technique recommended by financial experts is visualization. Visualization is the act of picturing what you want until it becomes true. Like affirmation, visualization is an exceptionally powerful mental exercise that can have astonishing results. An example of how to use visualization is to imagine what life will be like once you reach millionaire status. Let your mind create the scene. To enhance the experience, you must be detailed and specific. Engage all your senses so that you see, touch, hear, smell, and taste what it is to be a millionaire. Not only does picturing yourself as a millionaire bring this reality to you faster, but it prepares you in advance for how to function as a millionaire so there are few surprises or challenges when you get there.

All millionaires know that affirmations and visualizations used together are powerful tools that can radically change your life. Use the following principles to incorporate affirmations and visualizations to make your dream of becoming a millionaire a reality.

Principle #44

Incorporate positive affirmations into your daily routine.

※

Positive thinking does not come naturally to most of us. People must train themselves to view things in a positive light. Use positive affirmations to reprogram negative thoughts. Instead of telling yourself, "I will never be rich," think, "I am on the path to wealth already." Over time, the moments will add up to a powerful collection of positive hours, and eventually, days. Not only will affirming the positive put you on the path to wealth, it will also extend your life. A recent study by researchers at the Mayo Clinic found that people who think positively live 19 percent longer than those who do not.

Principle #45

Surround yourself with images of wealth.

Your mind processes millions of images every day. What an opportunity to transform your mindset! The images you see each day are like data fed into a computer. Your brain is the computer — be sure to upload it with images of wealth. Make your home a place of inspiration toward wealth. You can do this by hanging in prominent places messages such as "I will become a millionaire" along with photos and paintings of what wealth means to you.

Principle #46

Tell yourself you will become a millionaire. Then tell yourself again. And again.

An affirmation is the repetition of something that exists or is true. Your truth is that you will become a millionaire. In order to believe this truth you must work from the inside out. Do this by convincing yourself you *will* become a millionaire. Not that you want to become one — but that you *will* become one. For this to work, use repetition to condition your mind to accept this eventual reality. Famed author of *Think and Grow Rich*, Napoleon Hill, wrote, "Any idea, plan, or purpose may be placed in the mind through repetition of thought." Once in the mind, action is not far behind!

Principle #47

Write your life story
as you want it to read.

Recognize that your life is entirely up to you. To fully feel the power of your life story, write out your biography up to this point. Writing about your past will help you both understand your present and predict your future. Do not write the final chapter, because this will impose limits on how successful you can become. In some chapter in the second half of the book, write the words, "I became a millionaire at the age of _____." Be sure to choose an age within 5 to 10 years of your current age.

Principle #48

Allow yourself to revise your life story as things change.

❋

Millionaires know one secret to success is flexibility. In fact, wealthy people roll with changes instead of being crushed by them. Apply this idea to your life story. Once you have written your biography, revise it as circumstances change. Add chapters to the end, because you should always be reaching beyond where you are. For example, when you're writing as a millionaire, add chapters for when you become a billionaire. Keep your limits loose and allow for room to grow. As author T. Harv Eker writes, "Rich people constantly learn and grow. Poor people think they already know."

Principle #49

Take your mind on a million-dollar vacation.

For just for a few minutes each day, sit quietly and shut out everything but your million-dollar vacation. Allow your mind to drift to the Caribbean or to a castle in Scotland. Let yourself taste the foods you would order and the wine you would drink. Notice how all worries of bills and day-to-day life drift away. Allowing your mind to drift to luxurious destinations gives you incentive to keep on track toward your goal of becoming a millionaire. Doing so often enough will get your mind used to the feeling and you will begin to crave the real experience, which will keep you motivated to become a millionaire.

Principle #50

Think of positive thoughts like a boomerang.

The law of attraction states that energy attracts similar energy. Therefore, if you send out positive thoughts to God or the universe, these thoughts will boomerang back to you with what you asked for. This may sound simple, but it takes a lot of work to create such energy. You must first identify that you wish to become a millionaire. Second, you must focus and practice as if you really deserve to be wealthy. Third, you must think and feel as if you are already a millionaire. Finally, you must be completely open and ready to receiving what you've asked for, no matter how it manifests.

Principle #51

Think only wealthy thoughts.

The desire to become a millionaire must be all-consuming. In order to stay this focused, you must start with your thoughts. In fact, most, if not every single thought you have, should be somehow related to becoming a millionaire. So, be sure to think only in terms of wealth. For example, several financial experts have suggested that focusing on what you cannot afford causes you to stay broke. On the other hand, if you zero-in on and adopt the qualities that millionaires possess, such as entitlement and feeling empowered, you dramatically increase your ability to be lucrative.

Principle #52

Use visualization techniques to push you toward wealth.

In 2006, Rhonda Byrne's book *The Secret* became a bestseller overnight. But the book's main premise is no secret at all. *The Secret* simply says the key to happiness, wealth, and success is to picture yourself as a happy, wealthy, and successful person. Use visualization techniques to achieve this. For example, write yourself a check for a million dollars and stick it on your bathroom mirror. Look at it every day. This will not only encourage you to seek out lucrative opportunities but will remind you of your worth.

HARNESSING THE POWER
OF AUTOSUGGESTION

In 1913, French psychologist and pharmacist Émile Coué introduced a type of psychotherapy called "optimistic autosuggestion." This self-help technique was based on the idea that a person could overcome their situation by changing their outlook via subconscious manipulation. Coué found he was able to help his patients overcome various maladies by practicing autosuggestion on them. Coué's most famous suggestion was, "Every day, in every way, I'm getting better and better." He discovered that the success of his patients was directly tied to positive, healing messages he delivered to them when they were in a relaxed, almost hypnotic state. He found that repetition of the statements was necessary for it to work. Of course, the suggestions had to be based in reality. In other words, a patient without limbs could not grow new legs despite how many times he was told he could. But as long as the suggestions were grounded in reality, Coué found that he could cure a variety of mental and physical conditions and was lauded for his outstanding success rate for common ailments such as asthma and anxiety.

In time, it became clear that autosuggestion could be used on oneself to better one's own financial circumstances. Autosuggestion became popularized in this way in Napoleon Hill's 1937 inspirational classic *Think and Grow Rich*. Hill asserted that when desiring wealth you ought to "see and feel money in your hands." He wrote, "Through repetition of this procedure, you voluntarily create thought habits which are favorable to your efforts to [change] desire into its monetary equivalent." Hill's treatise on becoming wealthy relied heavily on his readers' use of autosuggestion to make themselves feel worthy of riches.

Coué, Hill, and contemporary experts agree that your ability to succeed is 100 percent affected by your state of mind. In other words, if you do not feel you deserve to prosper, you won't. Autosuggestion is a relatively simple way to change your reality from the inside out. It is essentially convincing yourself to become ready for wealth and success. The following principles offer straightforward methods to ease you into the practice of autosuggestion. The steps are easy to follow and the results can be as grand as your suggestions.

PRINCIPLE #53

Practice mediation to get into a deeply relaxed state.

Put yourself into a state of relaxation so your mind can receive new messages and instructions. Meditation is a great way to put yourself in a deeply relaxed state. The simplest form of meditation is deep breathing. Start by removing all distractions. Go to a quiet room and sit in a comfortable position. Be mindful of your posture, and keep your back straight. Breathe deeply through your nostrils and allow your mind time to clear. Then, exhale one long, steady stream of air. Meditation takes practice but, with time, your busy brain will quiet down, allowing you to begin your autosuggestion program.

Principle #54

Listen to ambient music to prepare your mind to receive positive suggestions.

—— ✳ ——

Another effective way to prepare yourself for autosuggestion is to listen to low, ambient sounds or music. Ambient simply means "of the environment." Some people respond to simple drumbeats with flutes, while others find the sound of waves crashing or crickets to be relaxing. Musician Brian Eno states, "Ambient music must be able to accommodate many levels of listening attention without enforcing one in particular; it must be as ignorable as it is interesting." Combining ambient sounds with deep breathing exercises can put you into a deep state of relaxation that leaves your mind ready for autosuggestion.

Principle #55

Make positive suggestions while feeling relaxed, but aware.

While you want to be relaxed for autosuggestion, you do not want to be so relaxed that you zone out. As adults, it takes considerable effort to change our minds. So, for maximum results be absolutely sure that you are not too tired when you embark on the journey of changing your thought patterns. Make sure you remain alert and aware before you start replacing negative thoughts with positive ones. If sitting in a dark room causes you to doze off, keep the lights on. Only meditate when you are able to pay attention so your efforts are not wasted.

Principle #56

Use subliminal messages that support your goals.

Subliminal messaging is one of the most powerful forms of advertising and has been used in endeavors as far-ranging as selling soda to helping people quit smoking. Use subliminal messaging to get yourself to a place of wealth. There are several software programs that can help — they repeat positive affirmations that are not audible to you, but your mind will absorb them. Some programs allow you to record yourself making positive statements, while others use subliminal visual images. Look into which best suits your needs and expect to spend between $15 and a $100, or record yourself articulating your goals and play the recording every night as you sleep.

Principle #57

Experience wealth through sensation.

Autosuggestion experts agree that the most comprehensive method for changing the subconscious mind is to employ the senses. Focus your efforts on enlisting all 5 of your senses when visualizing yourself as wealthy. This can be done solely through visualization and concentration exercises. First, focus on a scene of wealth. See yourself standing in a large bank vault filled with cash. Feel the money in your hands. Smell the scent of ink and paper that fills the room. Hear yourself saying, "I am wealthy. All of this money is mine." Imagine you're celebrating your wealth with an expensive glass of champagne — and visualize yourself tasting it.

PRINCIPLE #58

Choose your words carefully.

— ❈ —

It is important to choose the wording of your autosuggestions carefully, for the mind focuses on what it is most drawn to. For instance, avoid phrasing messages in the negative. Do not repeat to yourself, "I am not poor." Studies show that the mind gets stuck on "not" and "poor" and will disregard all the other words in the statement. Instead say, "I am wealthy." This pares the message down to its positive essence and gives the mind no room for negative interpretation. Autosuggestion can produce outstanding results if you stay focused on positive messages and block out the negatives.

Principle #59

Use the present tense to encourage identification with the experience.

When setting goals, many people are drawn to using the future tense. Common statements are "I will buy a house," or "I will be rich." However, this trains your mind to think that buying a house or becoming rich is always just out of reach. Instead, phrase your goals in the present tense. Think, "I own the home of my dreams," and, "I have vast riches." Present-tense statements encourage your brain to identify with the experience and to seek out opportunities that match this present sense of reality.

Principle #60

Make your internal voice the loudest one in the room.

When you embark on your path to wealth, you will inevitably come across naysayers. People who are threatened by your blossoming positivity and successful mindset will tell you that you are impractical, or that your efforts are a waste of time. The best way to combat those messages is to fall back on the positive state of being you've worked to create for yourself. Above all, never argue with naysayers. The most productive thing you can do is to smile and walk away while thinking, "I am wealthy. I am successful. I am strong."

Principle #61

Be consistent when using autosuggestion.

Autosuggestion is a technique that requires consistency in order to be effective. When you create the script of what to tell yourself, be sure it is consistent. How you receive these messages is less important than that you receive the same ones over time. For instance, programming your brain to believe you are deserving of wealth should have a limited number of statements to support it. Affirmations that fit are "I am rich," or "I deserve wealth." If your mind is going to learn to believe what you are telling it, you must tell it the same thing over and over until it is truly internalized.

Principle #62

Repeat after me.

No matter how you choose to employ autosuggestion, be sure to practice it often. Next to consistency, repetition is the most effective way to solidify your new wealthy mindset. As the great Muhammad Ali once said, "It's the repetition of affirmations that leads to belief. And once that belief becomes a deep conviction, things begin to happen." Indeed, all the great success stories of our time began with a state of mind. Because you likely have years of negative reinforcement to dismantle, you must practice autosuggestion as often as possible. Repeating positive affirmations until your brain drowns all negative thoughts is your greatest weapon against failure.

Developing Willpower
and Discipline

Walking the road to riches will require you to exhibit willpower and self-discipline. If in general you make good decisions, this may come easy for you. However, most of us fall short when it comes to our ability to control unnecessary or harmful urges. Part of what makes having willpower and self-discipline so difficult to cultivate is that it starts with making a decision — and then sticking to it. Some people find it difficult to make decisions, while others have trouble with follow-through. Either way, if you fall into either of these categories, you need to work on tightening up the reins that control your impulses.

Willpower is often associated with making difficult choices. Perhaps this is true, but it may help you to reframe your thinking and picture your life unfolding before you with no discipline. Obviously, it would become very difficult to get anything productive done without willpower. Laziness, procrastination, and fulfilling the desire for immediate satisfaction would prevent any long-term financial (or other) planning. When viewed in this light, developing willpower is seen as an important tool worth refining. Indeed, practicing restraint is self-affirming and character-building. It also teaches those around you that you can be counted on to make responsible decisions.

An important part of willpower is knowing when to say "no." There will be times when it will be extremely difficult. For instance, perhaps all your friends are going to Europe this winter, but you know you cannot afford it. Or, maybe the new large-screen high-definition television you've been wanting is for sale at your local electronics store. The easy road in both scenarios is to say "yes" and rack up credit-card debt. However, this goes against the grain of self-preservation, which is what willpower is all about.

If willpower is about making the right decision, then self-discipline is having the courage to stick to the decision no matter how challenging it becomes to do so. Developing self-discipline takes practice and lots of daily work. Enter into this work knowing that it will be difficult at times but worth it in the long run. Use the following principles to flex your self-control and remember that millionaires are made by their choices and ability to follow through with them.

Principle #63

Exercise every single day.

———————————————— ❋ ————————————————

Establishing an exercise routine — and sticking to it — is a necessary step in boosting your willpower and increasing your level of discipline. Be sure to get at least 30 minutes of physical activity every day. Even the busiest among us can make time for exercise. Some tips are to walk during your lunch break or to immediately head to the gym after work. Keep in mind that when you exercise, your body releases endorphins, which naturally elevate your mood and give you more energy. This good feeling will spill over into other areas of your life and help to keep you focused.

Principle #64

Avoid unnecessary or harmful habits.

❋

The guilt associated with engaging in behavior that you know is bad for you wreaks havoc on your psyche. Many of us end up in a downward spiral after sneaking a cigarette or downing a second donut. To avoid finding yourself in an out-of-control spiral, get to know what triggers behaviors that make you feel bad about yourself and avoid them. If you find that you always want a cigarette when you drink coffee, consider switching to tea. Take small steps away from damaging habits. As your self-control builds, you will want to make better choices in all parts of your life.

PRINCIPLE #65

Learn to delay instant gratification.

Delaying immediate gratification is the cornerstone of willpower and discipline. Indeed, our culture is increasingly built around the "need-it-now" mentality, which can be a dangerous and wasteful pitfall for the person who wants to become wealthy. Avoid falling into this trap by standing strong in the face of fleeting urges and spontaneous desires. Instead, achieve a balance between giving yourself what you need now and waiting for what you want later (or not at all). As author T. Harv Eker wrote, "Poor people choose *now*. Rich people choose *balance*." Eker became a millionaire in under 2½ years — you can do the same by delaying instant gratification.

Principle #66

Work even when you don't feel like it.

———————— ✳ ————————

Having a computer at your desk affords us the chance to goof off at work while still appearing busy. Though you may be fooling your boss, you are not fooling yourself. Such behavior teaches your subconscious mind that it is okay to opt out of responsibility. Remember that achieving genuine discipline requires total commitment. If you feel yourself losing interest at work, take a break. Tell yourself, "I am taking a break so that I may return focused and ready to work." When you return to your desk, get back to work. Regularly practicing such discipline is invaluable to your self-esteem and overall sense of pride.

Principle #67

Break it down to get it down.

At times we are each faced with a task that seems so overwhelming our mind shuts down at the sheer thought of it. Perhaps for you this is what happens when you think of all the steps required to become a millionaire. If so, you are not alone. In fact, subconscious resistance to getting started is the number one reason people cite for giving up on their dreams. To keep your dreams alive, learn to break down large tasks or goals into smaller, more manageable steps. By tackling things in small doses, you can dismantle your mental block and find your will to act.

Principle #68

Practice self-discipline by engaging in disagreeable activities.

Exercise your self-discipline by engaging in activities you would ordinarily shy away from. This is an excellent way to flex your discipline and build your willpower. Find ways each day to practice. For example, let cars cut in front of you on your morning commute. Give up your seat on the train. Let the person with more groceries get in line ahead of you. Think of these as self-discipline-strengthening exercises, like when you lift weights and your muscles get stronger. Achieving willpower and discipline is possible only by overcoming resistance to things you don't want to do.

Principle #69

Avoid procrastination — it is the kiss of death to success.

Never were truer words written than the proverb "Never put off until tomorrow what you can do today." Indeed, procrastination has been the death of many a plan and dream. Procrastination eats away at willpower and self-discipline because it allows you to let yourself off the hook from responsibility. To avoid this trap, once you have established goals, get to work on them today. Waiting for tomorrow will most assuredly keep you from ever taking action, because the time may never feel right to get moving.

Principle #70

Don't be lazy!

✳

Laziness, or sloth, is one of the seven deadly sins in Christianity. In the Bible, Jesus likens laziness to wickedness, and Ecclesiastes 10:18 states that laziness leads to poverty. These are some heavy indictments against laziness! Throughout history, wise (and wealthy) people have recognized that laziness is self-indulgent and useless behavior. If you allow yourself to be lazy, you waste precious minutes of your life and stunt your potential. So, the next time you feel drawn to laze upon the couch, employ some self-discipline. Instead, go for a walk. Revisit and update your goals or biography. Pay your bills, or start an online class that will increase your skill set.

Principle #71

Know that perseverance leads to excellence.

When you are faced with an obstacle, your response to it will make or break you. Choosing to persevere instead of giving up is a key component to being successful. There is no better example for this than 7-time Tour de France winner Lance Armstrong. In 1996, Armstrong was diagnosed with testicular cancer that had spread to his lungs, abdomen, and brain. While undergoing chemotherapy, he chose to continue his training. Armstrong went on to not only beat cancer but win the 1999 Tour de France. Armstrong is proof that perseverance and discipline are primary factors in overcoming adversity and achieving success.

Principle #72

Practice willpower because it feels good to say "no" sometimes.

It is empowering to be at a point in life when you can set boundaries and say "no." This is more difficult for younger adults who often have trouble making decisions that separate them from the pack. A person in his 20s may continue to stay out late, even if he doesn't want to, just to be with the "in" crowd. However, the same man in his 30s may gather a great deal of self-respect from saying "no" to his buddies and heading home to prepare for the upcoming workday. Making such decisions exhibits maturity along with self-discipline.

Acquiring Knowledge

Acquiring the necessary knowledge for making your goals and dreams a reality is where you will gain great advantage in life, particularly in your pursuit of becoming a millionaire. Ideally, you should expand your knowledge base over the course of your lifetime — in other words, put no limits on what and how much you can learn.

The level of education that you obtain is completely within your control. Financial aid and student loans make formal education possible for just about anyone. If you are averse to pursuing a higher degree, know it will absolutely increase your chance of becoming a millionaire. Statistics show that an individual's net worth (the amount by which their assets exceed their liabilities) is directly proportional to his education level. Consider the following: On average, the net worth for those without a high school diploma is $20,600; with a high school diploma, $68,700; with some college, $69,300; and with a college degree, $226,100.

If you do not have time to attend classes in person, there are numerous online courses available — and don't forget about such resources as the public library and community continuing-education courses.

Since knowledge is so accessible, there is no excuse for not finding the answers you need. In fact, start now by reading every book you can get your hands on regarding building your personal financial portfolio. Once you start reading about how to accumulate wealth, you will find that many of the ideas start to blend together or seem to repeat themselves. This is not because the authors lack imagination — it is because there is a basic formula to becoming rich. It is simple and you already know it: *earn more than you spend.* However, learning how to apply this formula to your life is where you need to be as educated as possible. Being highly educated allows you to gain the necessary skills and technical knowledge that increase your earning potential.

It may also be helpful to expand your idea of what it means to acquire knowledge. Keep in mind that true learning happens in every moment of every day. Acquiring knowledge means paying attention to lessons as they present themselves. As you tune in to the constant flow of information available, actively seek ways to achieve your goals; be receptive to the sights, sounds, smells, tastes, and tactile quality of the world and its many experiences. In this way you are educating yourself. Make sure to incorporate the following simple principles to help guide you toward acquiring the knowledge necessary for meeting your goals.

Principle #73

Read books written by, about, or for millionaires.

The fastest road to becoming a millionaire is already paved, so don't waste time trying to reinvent the wheel. There are hundreds of books written by, about, and for millionaires. Most are willing to tell the world the secret of their success, so tap into this accessible resource. Becoming a millionaire is going to take work and time. In fact, it will become your full-time job *and* hobby. Read such authors as David Bach, Loral Langemeier, Napoleon Hill, and T. Harv Eker to help you internalize your millionaire mindset and learn practical tips for action.

Principle #74

Listen to highly successful people.

The human brain is able to process up to 50,000 thoughts per day. Some of these thoughts are more valuable and memorable than others. Replace less valuable thoughts with applicable ideas. Listen to wealthy people talk about how they became rich. If you feel comfortable, approach the head of your company and ask him or her for advice on how to succeed. Listen to motivational CDs during your commute and while at home. Attend conferences and readings held by your favorite speakers. Absorb the success of others for inspiration and instruction.

Principle #75

Learn how to invest.

※

Even the smartest among us can be intimidated by the ins and outs of investing. However, to dramatically increase your wealth and plan for retirement, you must learn how to invest wisely. There are online courses available that teach the technical side of investing. But if you do not intend on becoming a stockbroker or financial advisor, you may want to purchase books on investing or visit a free website, such as www.investopedia.com. Spend as much time as you can educating yourself on the basics of investing so that you may start growing your wealth as soon possible.

Principle #76

Take a finance class.

All community colleges and major universities offer a basic finance class. It is advisable for you to enroll in one, or in an online course, so that you may learn the founding principles of economics. Demystifying the various elements of business is sometimes enough to jump-start your self-confidence. On-site classes are always preferable because you can network with people who have similar interests, but online courses will provide you knowledge and convenience. Keep in mind that every minute you spend educating yourself about financial matters is an investment in your future life as a millionaire.

Principle #77

Learn the language of money.

———————————— ✳ ————————————

When some people hear details about the Dow Jones Industrial, they get immediately and completely lost. Many of us understand that this is a market in which stock is traded but do not understand the process. To further your understanding of investing, saving, and economics in general, it is a good idea to familiarize yourself with the language of money. There are many new words you should learn if you plan to manage your own investment accounts: annuity, equity, bonds, and market-value are just a few. Many books will spell out these concepts for you, or visit www.teachmefinance.com for definitions.

Principle #78

Learn a foreign language.

In the modern global economy it is increasingly important to speak a foreign language if you want to get to the top of your profession. In fact, speaking a second language vastly increases your earning potential; one recent survey found that 30 percent of hiring managers considered having a second language "very important" when selecting potential candidates. So, investigate which languages are commonly spoken in your business. For instance, if your company deals with workers in San Diego, get fluent in both English and Spanish. A secondary benefit to knowing another language is that it widens your networking potential.

Principle #79

Become tech savvy.

————————— ❈ —————————

It seems impossible that in this era there could be anyone left who doesn't know how to use a computer — but they are out there. If you are uncomfortable with computers, don't panic. Many resources are available to help you. First, it is imperative for you to become tech savvy; there are few industries that don't rely on computers for record keeping, research, and business transactions. The more you know about computers, the more efficient your work will be. This also applies to other tech tools like cell phones, BlackBerries, and other PDAs. People with computer skills will be in demand for the foreseeable future. Make sure you are one of them.

Principle #80

Study current real estate trends.

— ※ —

Most of America's wealthiest people became rich through their dealings in real estate. As you learn how to increase your earnings and invest your money, real estate will inevitably be featured in your research. Note that billionaire Donald Trump became a millionaire when he was still in college while working for his father's real estate company. Also, 46 people on *Forbes* magazine's list of billionaires made their fortunes in real estate. Start now to learn everything you can about real estate trends.

Principle #81

Read constantly.

———————— ✳ ————————

Always have something on hand to read. Studies show that people who read a lot have higher vocabularies and superior comprehension over those who rarely read. Carry a book around with you at all times in case you find yourself waiting for an appointment or standing in line. Sign up to have *The Wall Street Journal* and *The New York Times* Sunday service so you can keep up with news and economic and real estate trends. Remember to look up unfamiliar words and to talk about what you've read to better absorb the material.

Principle #82

Join a networking group.

✳

Networking is a fantastic way to meet other motivated people who have different skill sets from your own. These groups often allow only 1 person from each profession to encourage diversity and maximize the referral system. Establishing such relationships at the early stage of your wealth-building can come in handy later. For instance, if your goal is to earn your first million by selling your product online, it would behoove you to be connected to a computer technician. Also, don't be afraid to ask lots of questions. Remember that everyone else is there to make connections and learn, too.

CREATING A PLAN

Create a plan of action to focus your efforts on becoming a millionaire and get immediate results. Though you may be tempted to feel overwhelmed by the task, keep in mind that planning can start with a basic outline. Simply detail the steps you must take to achieve your goals. Following a plan allows you to keep track of your accomplishments, which helps motivation levels remain high. It also allows you to articulate what you want to achieve and how to achieve it. In fact, coming up with your plan of attack can be quite invigorating. But above all, it is impossible to succeed at whatever you intend to do without a plan. It is for this reason that it is often said, "The man who fails to plan, plans to fail."

Note that all good plans are grounded in realistic expectations. They are directed toward the successful completion of long-term objectives. The most effective plans are detailed, yet flexible. They should always be well-researched. They should also follow a certain time frame. Your plan should be a combination of long- and short-term aspirations.

Many people have been asked by a potential employer, "Where do you see yourself in 5 years?" When creating your plan, ask yourself this question and base your plan on the answer. Starting with the 5-year model will give you a point of reference and make it easier to add to it. You may then expand your plan to 10, 20, and 35 years with relative ease. When building your plan for wealth, be sure to incorporate the following simple principles in your research.

Principle #83

Know what you want to accomplish.

When creating a plan of action, clearly articulate your goals. First, have a brainstorming session. Let ideas flow without interruption or judgment. Be sure to write down whatever comes to mind. The next step is to tighten up the looser ideas. For instance, a more specific version of "start a business" would be "own my own bookstore within 10 years." Making goals specific helps you to zero in on what you want to accomplish. Then, start thinking about how to achieve them.

Principle #84

Write a personal mission statement.

— ❈ —

Crafting a plan for wealth involves generating an idea of who you are and what you intend to do with your life. Writing a mission statement will help pinpoint where you should focus your efforts. Your mission statement should clearly state the things in life that are most important to you — things that motivate you to go from one step to the next. It should also reflect goals based on these values. Your mission statement should be motivational, easy to understand, and action-oriented. It should appeal to you personally and emotionally.

Principle #85

Research what others have done.

---　✳　---

Half the battle to wealth is figuring out what steps to take to acquire it. Sitting down with your list of aspirations can be very daunting. This is especially true if becoming a millionaire is at the top. Your first thought will likely be, "Where do I begin?" The best way to orient yourself is to research the steps other millionaires have taken. Remember, there is no shame in copying successful behavior. In fact, it would be foolish to try to forge your own path to riches when there are so many well-documented versions of the tried-and-true road to achievement.

Principle #86

Articulate your short-term goals.

To jump-start your plan, keep a list of short-term goals. These can be things you can accomplish on a daily or weekly basis that bring you closer to wealth. Some can be easy money-saving tasks, such as sending in a rebate or switching your car insurance to get a lower rate. Others can be activities you've been meaning to do but haven't gotten around to, such as reading a book on a millionaire you admire or signing up for a finance class. Cross items off your list as you complete them. This will give you an immediate sense of accomplishment and keep you motivated to work toward your larger goals.

Principle #87

Articulate your long-term goals.

— ✳ —

Consider what your long-term goals are. Do you want to get an advanced degree? Start a lucrative online business? Make your first million in the stock market? Own a beautiful home? Travel to a ritzy destination? Write your long-term goals down and put them in a highly visible place. Viewing the milestones you have yet to reach will remind you that you do have a plan and that it is to fulfill these goals.

Principle #88

Make goals measurable.

Loose goals such as "I want to be successful" are immeasurable and therefore frustrating, because they are not specific. So when creating your goals, articulate measurable ones that can be clearly reached. For example, if you want to save more money this year, write, "I want to save $4,000 by December 31." Then, make a list of the amount you plan to deposit each month. After each transaction, put a check mark next to the month and amount. As you mark off the months, be sure to add up the sum of your deposits so you can track how close you are to your goal.

Principle #89

Create a timeline for action.

※

Timelines are a must when outlining a plan of action. Without deadlines and time frames, even the best plans tend to drag on indefinitely. Designating specific time frames is universally recommended by financial experts to reach goals. For instance, if you plan to invest money in stock for a particular company, indicate a cutoff date for when to accomplish this. Write, "I will invest $1,000 in Company A by May 1." Do this for each of your goals. Next, create a "goal calendar" where you write down these dates. Hang it in a prominent place; this will keep your deadlines at the forefront of your mind.

Principle #90

Make an action book
with a table of contents.

Organization is important for keeping your plans alive. A good way to accomplish this is to create an "action book." Your action book should include a page for each of your goals. On each page, list the steps necessary to reach the goal and the date by which you intend to accomplish each step in the plan. Leave room for notes so you can make changes as necessary. Give your action book a table of contents with page numbers for easy reference. Get creative with your action book by writing an inspirational message that relates to the particular goal at the top of the page.

Principle #91

Make sure your plan is realistic.

Business tycoon Warren Buffett once said, "I don't look to jump over 7-foot bars; I look around for 1-foot bars that I can step over." Buffett was commenting on the importance of being realistic when you make plans. Instead of resolving to earn an extra $200,000 this year, start by vowing to save an extra $5,000. Plan to buy nothing unless it is on sale by at least 30 percent. Remember that your goals should be things you are willing and able to do. Make goals that are possible to accomplish this week and build to the bigger goal with each passing week.

Principle #92

Revise your plan as necessary.

It is important to revisit your goals in light of shifting priorities and realties. For example: Let's say your goal is to pay off a credit card. Your plan includes increasing your income and paying $300 per month to creditors. During the time that you set these goals, you were working overtime and had extra cash to put toward debt. However, after company cutbacks, overtime was removed from the budget, and you became unable to make such high payments. At this point, you should revisit your goals and assess if your reality still fits your original plan. This ensures you are always in line with your plan, because your plan is fluid according to your current situation.

Principle #93

Get help enacting your plan.

Most of us prefer to accomplish our goals on our own. In fact, the "American way" is to try and solve our own problems and to pull ourselves up by our bootstraps. For some, it's a matter of privacy and for others a matter of pride. However, if you need help executing a section of your plan, you should absolutely seek support. You will find that many people you already know have the skills to help you. It is important to remember that every single millionaire has enlisted the help of people in their network to achieve their goals.

TAKING ACTION

*T*hink and *Grow Rich* author Napoleon Hill wrote that having all the knowledge in the world won't do you any good unless you use it. Indeed, to accomplish your plan of becoming a millionaire, you must take action. After all, money isn't going to magically appear in your bank account. The good news is that there are several steps you can take each day that will bring you closer to your goals. If you identified what your goals are and crafted a plan to reach them, you have already taken the preliminary steps. Everything that comes after serves to support what you have already determined to accomplish.

One way to ensure that you reach your goals is to ask yourself daily, "What 5 things will I do today that will bring me closer to my goals?" Indeed, beginning your day this way reminds you that you have a larger purpose. When you come up with your 5 things, write them down in a notebook to carry with you. As you complete a task, mark it off. If at the end of the day you find you have not completed all 5, don't admonish yourself. Instead, simply carry over whatever was left on your list for the next day.

Should you get discouraged, remember that it takes courage to reach your goals. All of us know the person who constantly talks about the trip they plan to take or the move they plan to make, yet they never actually follow through. Taking action on grand plans takes courage and perseverance, and you should congratulate yourself for being fearless in an area where so many have faltered. As Ralph Waldo Emerson once wrote, "Don't be too timid and squeamish about your actions. All life is an experiment." So, get ready to embark on your great experiment. Use the following simple principles to kickstart your dreams of becoming a millionaire into action.

Principle #94

Enter into a success contract with yourself.

After you have articulated your goals, write out a success contract with yourself. Most of us are more inclined to act when we feel legally obligated, so take this contract seriously. Download free versions of real contracts at www. businessnation.com/library/forms and then personalize the terms of the agreement. This will help you to stick to your goals. Create consequences if you renege on any part of your commitments. An example is to make yourself pay a $50 fine to your savings account each time you violate the terms of the contract.

Principle #95

Follow through with your plans.

—— ✳ ——

All the planning in the world will not get you an inch closer to your goals unless you actually follow through with them. So, after you have crafted a plan for yourself, make a formal commitment to following it. Do this by having a commitment ceremony in which you read your plan aloud to family or friends who can hold you accountable to it. As racecar driver Mario Andretti once said, "Desire is the key to motivation, but it's determination and commitment to an unrelenting pursuit of your goal — a commitment to excellence — that will enable you to attain the success you seek."

Principle #96

Develop a savings plan.

Saving money is integral to your family's well-being, so start right now. If you have trouble getting motivated, consider the following: According to *The Smart Student Guide to Financial Aid*, "Parents should try to save at least one-third to half the projected costs of their child's college education. Ideally the savings plan should be established when the child is born, but it is never too late to start saving. To reach $35,000, you would need to contribute $25.12 per week for 17 years to an account that earns 5 percent interest." Clearly, there is no time like the present to start building up your family's savings account.

Principle #97

Make leisure time count.

Make sure to keep your eyes and ears open at all times, because you never know when something fruitful may come along. In fact, the next time you are at the dog park and someone tries to strike up a conversation about business, stay and participate. Two people talking often attract the attention of others, and before you know it you're networking and exercising your dog at the same time. *Forbes* magazine highly recommends this approach: "Networking during leisure activities works because people are not consciously thinking about their jobs. Your shared interests allow you to naturally get to know someone personally before you know them professionally."

Principle #98

Share your goals with people you trust.

———————————————— ✳ ————————————————

Enlist the help of family and friends as you work toward your dream of becoming a millionaire. They will provide a critical support network that will cheer you on in times of success and hold you up in times of challenge. This support network should be different than the one you will build out of business contacts. Your network of family and friends can be trusted with your fears, challenges, insecurities, and private information in a way that business contacts cannot. Use this network of people you trust especially when you are faced with making a difficult decision or need motivation.

Having Patience

Americans are perhaps the most impatient people on earth. Our increasingly convenient and online culture has trained us to be unaccustomed to having to wait. In a matter of seconds, we can pay our bills, order food, send correspondence, and shop. Yet, despite all of these advantages, Americans report the lowest level of happiness than any other industrialized country. According to reporter John Lanchester in *The New Yorker* magazine, "Looking at the data from all over the world, it is clear that, instead of getting happier as they become better off, people get stuck on a 'hedonic treadmill': their expectations rise at the same pace as their incomes, and the happiness they seek remains constantly just out of reach." An argument can therefore be made that we don't need more money or convenience; perhaps what we need instead is more *patience*. John Quincy Adams once said, "Patience and perseverance have a magical affect before which difficulties disappear and obstacles vanish." It is to this end you must learn to have patience if you wish to fulfill your goal of becoming a millionaire.

Having patience is a much needed — and rarely practiced — skill in western society. Interestingly, patience is a virtue in all of the major world religions, including Judaism, Christianity, Islam, and Buddhism, which all have tenets related to it. And, when asked, most people state they are affiliated with a particular religion, or at least claim to be spiritual. Yet, how many times have you been screamed at in traffic or been given dirty looks at the post office? In such moments, patience seems to be one of the first spiritual tenets to fall by the wayside. If you find yourself succumbing to impatience, perhaps it is time to cultivate your spiritual side. For the less spiritual among us, a little perspective is all we need to have patience for the day-to-day annoyances. Indeed, looking at the bigger picture can put whatever small annoyance is causing you to be impatient in perspective.

Finally, it will be impossible for you to become a millionaire without exercising patience. You absolutely can become a millionaire if you set your mind to it, but this goal will not be accomplished overnight. Nor will it be without its trials, challenges, and setbacks. Therefore, cultivating a deep sense of patience is essential to weathering the bumpy path to success. Use the following principles to develop a sense of patience that you can fall back on when times get tough.

Principle #99

Remember that Rome wasn't built in a day.

Earning your first million will take time. You will need patience to see your dream through to the end. Even though it may feel as though you're not making progress toward your goals, remember that your actions are not wasted. Everything you do, no matter how small, builds toward your ultimate objective. Avoid rushing through the steps it takes to become financially independent. If you find yourself starting to feel impatient, remember this Chinese proverb: "One moment of patience may ward off great disaster. One moment of impatience may ruin a whole life."

Principle #100

Learn patience by setting smaller goals.

---　✳　---

Many of us want to immediately reach our goals and have little patience for the steps that must be taken to get from A to Z. Luckily, this scenario has an easy fix — break larger goals down into smaller, easily accomplished steps. Large undertakings often fail because people don't give themselves a realistic time frame or write out what they want to accomplish. Instead, spread your project or goal into manageable steps so that you tackle small bits and see the fruits of your labor.

Principle #101

Blow off impatience.

---※---

An excellent way to cultivate the skill of having patience is to practice deep breathing. Deep breathing exercises are the key component in de-escalating volatile situations, yet 90 percent of humans rarely, if ever, practice them. In fact, most people take quick, shallow breaths when they become impatient. Next time you are faced with a stressful situation, remember that breathing deeply increases oxygen content in the blood, decreases blood pressure and heart rate, and immediately lowers stress levels. Once you are relaxed and feel rational, you will find it is much easier to remain patient.

PRINCIPLE #102

Use patience to override the urge for instant gratification.

In our online world where you can access almost anything you need 24 hours a day, it is not surprising that we have developed an increasingly impatient culture. Many of us hate waiting for what we want so much that we constantly engage in activities that provide instant gratification. We shop online at 10 p.m., run to the 7-11 for ice cream at 2 a.m., or get our oil changed in 10 minutes. We are taught less and less to cultivate patience. This is not realistic or healthy. You will find you need patience to obtain your goal of becoming a millionaire. Train yourself to wait.

Principle #103

Count to 10.

It can help to count to 10 in a situation that requires extreme patience. Get back in touch with this tried-and-true method for generating patience. Counting is a very effective tool to rely on when you find yourself on the verge of making an irrational comment or decision. It breaks up destructive thought patterns and lures your focus from whatever incident made you impatient to begin with.

PRINCIPLE #104

Learn the art of compromise.

— ✳ —

Practicing yoga regularly can center you squarely in the present, helping to combat the frantic need to rush ahead that comes from being impatient. Studies show that yoga relieves anxiety, improves memory, and increases mental clarity and processing. It also improves self-esteem and deepens your ability to remain patient during frustrating situations. This is the result of being more relaxed and more tuned in to enjoying all of life's moments — even the annoying ones.

PRINCIPLE #105

Enjoy the journey.

— ✳ —

Impatience usually stems from our desire to find the quickest route from where we start to our destination. The construction of freeways, bridges, and tunnels are founded on this principle. Yet, how much do you enjoy the detour that leads you away from the freeway and through the back roads? Wise thinkers upon their deathbeds have said that they finally realized that the journey *was* the destination. Don't become so focused on skipping to the end that you miss all of the experiences that get you there. This is the space in which the best parts of life often unfold.

BUILDING A SUPPORTING NETWORK

Think of your goal to become a millionaire as a house you plan to build. You know that you cannot build an entire house by yourself, so you will need to enlist the help of others. This is where networking comes in. If you are the architect of your house, then the people with whom you network are the electricians, plumbers, decorators, and painters. Building a supporting network, then, is a way to give your goals foundation, substance, and decoration. Indeed, when trying to accomplish something as grand as becoming a millionaire, going it alone is not only difficult and unnecessary but foolish. As Ringo Starr famously sung, "I get by with a little help from my friends." Indeed, the people you meet through networking may become some of your closest friends.

Some shy away from networking because they view it as uncomfortable, forced, or only intended for a particular type of businessperson. But networking is no longer an early morning boys club. Indeed, men and women from all types of professions engage in both professional and social networking to increase their business prospects and to broaden their social horizons. Statistics show that women are the fastest-growing demographic in networking. A recent study conducted by a major financial firm found that women are actually better at networking than men because they are more likely to strike up conversations with others. They also engage in hobbies that create intimacy, such as knitting or doubles tennis.

In this day and age, there are many interesting and enjoyable ways to network. When done right, networking is an effortless and natural part of your daily life. It is simply the process of making yourself, your skills, and your career goals known to the people you interact with every day. This doesn't mean that you should rattle off a list of your qualifications to everyone you meet. It does mean you should find ways to inject tidbits about who you are and what you do when you interact with people. Let friends know you are looking for a new job. Chat with those in line with you at the bank about what they do — perhaps your careers intersect. Keep in touch with coworkers after they leave your company so you stay up to date with things going on in the industry. Let family know you're looking for an investment opportunity. Each of these is an example of making your goals known to a wide range of people who could be in the position to help you reach them. It may not be clear in the moment how these relationships will benefit you — and not every one will. But the key is to start a conversation, thereby creating the potential for a relationship to develop. Use the following simple principles for suggestions on how to increase your chances of success by building a solid support network.

Principle #106

Realize that you already have over 50 contacts.

---- ❋ ----

Without even realizing it, it is likely that you already know many people who can help you reach your goals. Make a list of your contacts. First, list personal contacts and divide this list into family, friends, and neighbors. Next, list other personal contacts — include your dentist, your lawyer, the people you know from social or religious clubs, and others. Then, list professional contacts such as people you have worked with, worked through, worked for, or given work to. List customers, clients, consultants, even competitors. Tally up the names of the people in all the different categories. You will likely be surprised by the extent of your network.

Principle #107

Network with those who complement your profession.

When networking, seek out people with different skills from you to maximize the areas in which you can be successful. You'll want to create a networking group with one member per industry. This is an excellent way to get people with different skill sets talking to one another. Include people you can have a give-and-take relationship with in your particular line of work. For example, if you are a realtor, it would behoove you to know a carpenter, landscaper, plumber, electrician, and a general handyman.

Principle #108

Use nontraditional venues to network.

Alternative networking venues are becoming increasingly popular. No longer are stuffy, early-bird meetings the norm. According to *The Wall Street Journal* article by journalist Perri Carrell, top women executives are pioneering creative ways to network that include making valuable contacts at book club meetings, nail and hair salons, hobby groups, and online chat rooms. Men too are making contacts when they are online, playing recreational sports, and engaging in a regular card group. Participating in such activities forges personal relationships that nearly always extend beyond the particular activity at hand.

Principle #109

Network for quality, not quantity.

—— ❈ ——

Anthropologists have found that for one person, a genuine social network — one in which you know the members and they know you — is limited to about 150 people. In fact, British anthropologist Robin Dunbar found there is a "cognitive limit to the number of individuals with whom any one person can maintain stable relationships." So don't network just to network. Whittle down your contacts to the most fruitful ones. Coming away from an event with hundreds of business cards in hand means you've actually created more work for yourself, because you now must hunt through names of people you didn't get to know that well.

Principle #110

Make a statement with your business card design.

Business cards make it easy for others to get in touch. But increasingly, most people record contact information in their BlackBerries and other PDAs and throw away cards. To prevent your card from getting tossed, be creative with how you deliver your contact information. Use bold colors and graphics to accessorize your card. Placing pictures of fine art on your card will make its recipient less likely to throw it away. Also, end your emails with a signature line that contains your contact information, and enter your contact information in your cell phone to send it wirelessly.

Principle #111

Develop your own sound byte.

An important part of networking is being prepared to do it. You don't want to find yourself in the perfect networking situation and end up delivering a jumbled story about your background. Take the time to develop an introduction about yourself that lasts 1 to 2 minutes. Think of this as your own personal sound byte. It should concisely tell someone where you've come from and where you want to go. You can use your sound byte at dinner parties, interviews, conferences — anywhere there is an occasion to market yourself.

Principle #112

Treat everyone as a possible connection.

— ✳ —

Sometimes the best connections happen in the laid-back atmosphere of your daily life. Everyday errands at the doctor's office, the DMV, or the auto shop provide captive audiences in waiting rooms. Never hold anyone prisoner who isn't interested in chatting, but don't be afraid to strike up a casual conversation with a simple, "What do you do?" And if there ever was a reason to talk to the person sitting next to you on the plane, this is it. Even if he does not meet any of your needs, he might be able to provide insider knowledge on people or companies of interest to you.

Principle #113

Be the little fish in a big pond.

We often feel too intimidated to approach the president of our company or the speaker at a conference we attend. But future millionaires are not afraid of connecting with higher-ranking individuals. Remember, most people with power love to discuss how they came into their success. Ask specific questions about career choices they made. Eventually, he or she will ask you what your goal in attending the conference is or what you hope to gain from your employment with the company. Have your answers prepared ahead of time and be sure to thank the person for his or her time. And don't forget to hand out a business card.

Principle #114

Network outside of your comfort zone.

— ✳ —

Networking outside your specific field or area of interest can yield surprising results. You may get turned on to a subject you didn't know could interest you; you may also be able to work this new knowledge into conversations with others and build a bridge to your own needs. For example, you might discover from an outdoor-recreation specialist that you and your colleagues could benefit from a team-building retreat. A painter might introduce you to a new shade of red that will make a bolder statement on your website. Networking paired with your creativity will produce innovative ideas for reaching your goals.

PRINCIPLE #115

Build bridges, don't burn them.

When you leave a job, for whatever reason, be sure to leave on good terms; you never know when you will need to contact or utilize former employers or co-workers for recommendations or networking purposes. If you leave with an attitude of "good riddance," others will not be inclined to maintain a relationship with you. Wishing others well, providing your personal contact information, and making an effort to stay in touch are great ways to leave lines of communication open.

Principle #116

Be creative when you reward referrals.

When a person has given their word to someone else that you are the best they know for the job, show your appreciation. You can demonstrate gratitude to those who have passed your name along by writing a thank you note, taking them out for lunch, or sending a gift card or basket. If appropriate, offer your own services or skill set at a discounted rate to them. Make sure your reward is in direct proportion to the job you received — the person who gave a small referral should not be taken out for an extravagant dinner, and the person who gave a large referral should not be merely thanked.

Principle #117

Create your own website or blog.

Potential business contacts and clients will want to research your credentials and professional experience. Give them the resources to do so at any hour by creating a website. An effective website or blog should be regularly updated. It should express your knowledge, skills, and goals. Likewise, it is important to monitor what information already exists about you on the Internet. Employers increasingly do Web searches of people they consider hiring. It would be inappropriate for them to find compromising pictures or unprofessional blogs. Be sure that you present yourself in a manner that employers and colleagues will respect and admire.

Influencing People and Selling Your Ideas

Bill Clinton is famous for being the 42nd president of the United States, but he is equally famous for being highly skilled at influencing people and selling his ideas. Indeed, Clinton knows how to talk to people so well, those in his presence frequently report feeling under a spell while interacting with him. Even out of office, Clinton continues to use his talent for conversation to influence politicians to make decisions he supports and to persuade Americans to donate to campaigns and programs he believes in.

Knowing how to influence people is an acquired skill — many even regard it as an art. Peak performance expert Peter Murphy writes, "The art of conversation is a skill shared by most successful people. Good conversation promotes an image of self-confidence, intelligence, and wittiness." Thus, if you can carry on a good conversation, you can effectively position yourself to influence people and sell them your ideas.

Becoming an expert conversationalist will help you reach your goal of becoming a millionaire. Successful people often dazzle others with their words and thoughts and use their conversational powers to make connections that count. Dale Carnegie, author of *How to Win Friends and Influence People*, outlined several steps to develop conversational skills. They include:

- Be sure you are genuinely interested in others.
- Show them you are engaged by smiling often and by listening intently.
- Remember to use the person's name (because, according to Carnegie, "A person's name is to that person the sweetest and most important sound in any language").
- Encourage the other person to talk about himself and to discuss his motivations.
- Gain an idea of what drives a person and think in terms of their interests.

Perhaps the most important tip Carnegie offers is to make the other person feel genuinely valued. If you employ these tips in every interaction, you will quickly find that you have become the person who can make anyone listen and who can get things done. The following principles will provide you with several useful suggestions for improving the way you interact with others, thereby increasing your ability to influence others and sell them your ideas.

Principle #118

Know your audience.

Always be aware of the goals, needs, and backgrounds of the people with whom you speak. Indeed, understanding your audience constitutes the single most important aspect of having successful conversations. The time and effort spent on your conversation will be wasted if you do not take your audience into account. Think of what the person with whom you are speaking needs to know. Consider their vocabulary and the experience they have, and speak on that level. Your messages will be received more successfully than had you failed to consider your audience's interests and background.

Principle #119

Learn what motivates the people you seek to influence.

People are fueled by their own needs, not yours. So in order to influence them, you must first understand what is important to them. With this in mind, spending time discussing *your* desires and goals may not be the best hook for selling your ideas to others. Instead, ask questions to find out what makes others tick. Almost everyone you interact with will respond positively to this attention.

Principle #120

Listen intently.

An old Jewish proverb states, "No one is as deaf as the man who will not listen." Indeed, it is critical to become a good listener if you are to fulfill your goal of becoming a millionaire. Listening allows you to tap into the people, resources, and ideas around you. Good listeners never interrupt or cut the thoughts of others short. They never anticipate what a person is going to say and finish sentences. Listening in this way establishes trust and opens the lines of 2-way communication.

Principle #121

Ask critical questions.

— ✳ —

The best way to learn about someone who can help you become a millionaire is to ask good questions. Questions should follow the basic rules of journalism: who, what, where, when, why, and how. Ask follow-up questions to get detailed answers. If an answer is unclear to you, ask the person to clarify. Finally, always reciprocate when questions are asked of you. Never let someone ask you what you do or where you live without returning the question. To fail to return a question signals you are disinterested in learning about someone. It may also indicate you are self-centered, which puts off potential contacts.

Principle #122

Make real connections.

---- ✳ ----

Smart, successful people can always tell when someone is superficially interested in them. Indeed, most of us have been on the receiving end of this phenomenon — someone smiles and nods a lot but does not seem engaged in the conversation. They look around you as you talk and walk off the moment someone more interesting enters through the door. When developing business or personal relationships, seek genuine connections. Being fake offends people and causes them to discount you from any future dealings.

Principle #123

Learn to make small talk.

———————————— ✳ ————————————

Being conversational helps get the ball rolling and puts people at ease. Though subjects like the weather or traffic may seem superficial, the give and take of small talk is important for developing constructive dialogue when discussions get down to business. Also, knowing how to spark smart, interesting banter during otherwise "dead" spaces of time, such as waiting for a restaurant table, walking to a car, or taking the elevator, demonstrates to clients and coworkers that you are well-rounded and affable.

Principle #124

Appreciate all points of view.

———————— ✳ ————————

If you want to alienate those around you and become an island unto yourself, be sure to stick to your own point of view relentlessly. However, to make lasting connections, you should appreciate all points of view. This does not mean that you must condone behavior you find disagreeable or that you adopt another's mindset, it simply means that you acknowledge your ideas are not the only ones of value. Doing so makes others feel that you have regard for their opinion even when it differs from yours. This give and take opens the door for future commerce.

Principle #125

Master the art of public speaking.

❋

Public speaking is a skill you must learn to master if you want to become wealthy. A recent study found that 87 percent of a person's earning potential is directly linked to their speaking skills. Clearly, to be financially successful, you will need to learn the trick of the public-speaking trade. Enhancing your public-speaking skills will benefit more than your paycheck, however. Public speaking is about being able to communicate what you've learned. It's about being able to articulate your thoughts, feelings, and ideas and connecting them in ways that will inspire, persuade, inform, demonstrate, or commemorate.

Principle #126

Make eye contact.

A surefire way to influence people and sell your ideas is to make eye contact with whomever you're speaking. Looking in a person's eyes makes them feel acknowledged, valued, and heard. In fact, eye contact is so important, studies have shown that jurors rule in favor of defendants who maintain eye contact with them more often than with those who don't. If making eye contact does not come naturally to you, practice doing so with someone you already feel comfortable with. Finally, don't confuse making eye contact with staring; as a rule, socially appropriate eye contact is broken about every 3 seconds.

Principle #127

Present yourself as a person who makes things happen.

Everyone wants to give work to the person who knows how to make things happen, because he takes initiative to get things done. Become this person. Once you finish a project at work, don't wait to be assigned another one. Approach your boss and ask for more work. According to Bob Nelson, author of *Please Don't Just Do What I Tell You, Do What Needs to Be Done*, employees who take action and bring solutions to management are considered indispensable and are the first to be promoted and given raises. Becoming known as this person will carry you to professional success and becoming a millionaire.

PRINCIPLE #128

Become a great storyteller.

People love to listen to great orators and great storytellers are invited to more functions than they have time to attend. If you can tell a good story, you will have influence over everyone in the room. There are rules to storytelling. The first is to know your audience. If you are giving a speech at a nursing convention, don't tell your worst hospital experience. Another rule is to endear yourself to your audience, never alienate them. Also, have a story prepared, but don't recite it as if from memory. Leave room for back-and-forth spontaneity. This will make even the stalest story seem fresh.

Making the Right Decisions

In 1962, behaviorist Isabel Briggs Myers discovered that the human decision-making process depends on thinking and feeling, extroversion and introversion, judgment and perception, and sensing and intuition. This is called the Myers-Briggs Type Indicator (MBTI). When tested, those whose scores put them on the thinking, extroversion, sensing, and judgment side of the test tended to make decisions based on logic and analysis rather than emotion. However, recent scientific studies indicate that emotions actually play a larger role in decision making than cognition (perception). Both studies agree, however, that decision making is an involved process, and one that is critically important to master if a person wants to be successful.

Developing your decision-making skills is necessary to best position yourself for the millionaire life. In fact, making the right decisions is the first link in the chain of reactions that will get you from the place in which you are today to the wealth you'd like to hold tomorrow. Think of making good decisions as jumping from stepping stone to stepping stone without falling in the river. Each good step you take opens up a whole world of new choices; each bad decision leaves you soaking wet, or worse, drowning. With practice, you can improve your ability to make excellent decisions.

Getting better at making decisions in just one area of your life can vastly improve your overall quality of living. For example, even if you only get a handle on how to make good decisions in one area, such as your career, you will find this skill will spill over into areas in which you have more trouble making decisions, such as finances or shopping. Something to keep in mind is that *all* highly successful people are good decision makers. They find that making good decisions leads to enjoyment and self-confidence. Successful people enjoy the decision-making process itself and consider it to be an excellent and challenging way to constantly resharpen their minds and skills.

Above all, know decisions are not the end of an experience. Rather, they are bridges to new opportunities. Indeed, as Albert Camus wrote, "Life is the sum of all your choices." The following simple principles will help you make the right decisions to meet your goals and will leave you feeling satisfied with the sum of all your choices thus far.

Principle #129

Make choices that support your goals.

When working toward our goals, we may easily get derailed when a tempting situation presents itself. Though it is difficult to refrain from doing something you want in the moment, it is important to exhibit discipline. Examples are foregoing dinners out and weekend getaways when you are trying to save money for a house. It may feel like there is nothing you need more than to get out of town for a few days. But instead of spending $500 on a 3-day trip, put that money into your savings account. Continued commitment to your long-term goals is necessary if you plan to become wealthy.

Principle #130

Make every decision with good intentions.

In Buddhism, there are 3 "right intentions" that if followed will lead to diminished suffering. The first is the intention of resisting desire. The second is intention of good will. The third is the intention to do no harm. When you are making decisions, employ these 3 concepts to your process. Ask yourself if the decision you are about to make is based on desire, if it is in good will, and if it does any harm. Making good intentions part of the criteria for decision making will help you feel good about your choices.

Principle #131

Predict the outcome for all choices.

It is impossible to know for certain how a particular decision will turn out. It is, however, possible to predict what might happen. Predicting outcomes is a valuable tool when deciding between several options. For example, if you are deciding to pursue a higher degree, consider the outcome of your options. Law school is an expensive investment ($150,000 for 3 years) but can help increase your earning potential later in life. However, if you continue in your current job you will earn 3 years of salary and not go $150,000 into debt. Weighing these types of options will help you asses the outcome of your decision so you can make the right one.

Principle #132

Never make an important decision after 3 p.m.

Make meaningful decisions in the morning to early afternoon. Numerous studies have shown the mind to be most alert during the first few hours of the day. As the workday wears on, you become tired, sluggish, and tend to rush through decisions because you are not thinking clearly. So avoid making important decisions after 3 p.m. Consider this time the end of your day. If you have the option, always ask to sleep on big decisions. This gives you time to consider all factors and make an informed decision in the morning.

Principle #133

Be strategic.

Having a strategy is synonymous with developing a plan of action. A strategy serves as a guiding force when you are faced with decisions that have many factors. There are many issues to consider when planning a will, for instance. Who will be the guardians for your children? Who do you trust to hold power of attorney? Developing a strategy for attacking multifaceted decisions is absolutely necessary. In fact, don't allow yourself to make a single decision until you have a plan. First, figure out how you will make your selections and then begin to make your choices based on the criteria you've pre-established.

Principle #134

List the pros and cons before making a decision.

— ❊ —

The old standby in decision making is the pro/con list. Though it may seem obvious, it is a useful tool and should always factor into your strategy. List pros and cons on a sheet of paper and keep it handy so that you can add to it while in decision-making mode. Be sure to give certain factors more weight than others. For instance, when deciding which car to buy, gas mileage may be less important if you intend to continue to use public transportation for your commute to work.

Principle #135

Take responsibility for your decisions.

— ✳ —

Many of us try to find others to blame when a decision goes sour. However, millionaires never spend time blaming others for their mistakes. They accept it, learn from it, and move on to make better decisions in the future. Recognize that there is no bigger waste of time than regret. So, once you have made a decision, own it, accept it, and take responsibly for its outcome.

Principle #136

Make educated decisions.

Statistics show that the more important the decision, the less information a person gathers to inform it. Because some choices seem overwhelming and impending, people feel anxious researching the subject. Another reason people tend to not collect information regarding important decisions is that they do not want to be persuaded to change their minds. Ambivalence will not push you toward becoming a millionaire. Millionaires arm themselves with information before going out in the world, and they are not afraid of having their mind changed if the facts indicate that is appropriate.

Principle #137

Use your faith to help you make decisions.

Belonging to an organized religion or having a sense of spirituality can be an excellent asset when faced with a tough decision. From spirituality and religion, people derive a sense of right and wrong. They cultivate standards to live up to and a set of beliefs that guide them through each day. When faced with a difficult decision, turn to your faith to see what it has to say on the matter. Consult a spiritual authority or a holy book to see what advice is offered. After all, it is easy to make decisions when you know what your values are.

Principle #138

Go with your gut.

———————————— ✳ ————————————

Don't be afraid to rely on your gut when faced with difficult decisions — it has been scientifically proven as the best way to make them. A 2006 study published in the journal *Science* found that people who face a complex decision, such as what city to move to, choose poorly if they weigh positives and negatives too heavily. Instead, the best strategy is to gather all of the relevant information, such as the cost of living, the quality of school systems, the weather — and then put the decision out of mind for a while. When you must decide, go with what instinctively feels right. "It is much better to follow your gut," said lead researcher Ap Dijksterhuis on the subject.

Principle #139

Resist the urge to run your decisions past everyone you know.

Running your options past close friends or family is an excellent way to collect valuable opinions about the predicament in which you find yourself. But many of us feel compelled to tell everyone we meet about our agonizing decision whether to go back to school, sell our home, or relocate. In part, we do this to repeatedly hear out loud our choices, which is tempting, especially when we feel stuck. But by letting in too many voices, we end up discounting our own. So refrain from involving too many people in your decision-making process. As playwright Thornton Wilder wrote, "The more decisions you are forced to make alone, the more you are aware of your freedom to choose."

Principle #140

Don't be afraid to make emotional decisions.

Conventional wisdom tells us to keep emotions out of the decision-making process. But a fascinating 2006 brain-imaging study published in the journal *Science* suggests otherwise. Scientists found that the brain relies heavily on emotion over intellect in decision making. Researchers found this by asking 20 men and women to undergo brain scans while gambling $95. They found that the amygdala, a neural region that processes emotions such as fear, responded vigorously to each gambling decision. So don't suppress your emotions the next time you need to make an important decision; they will help guide you where you need to go.

Principle #141

Follow through after making a decision.

———————— ✳ ————————

Author William Pollard wisely stated, "It is not always what we know or analyzed before we make a decision that makes it a great decision. It is what we do after we make the decision to implement and execute it that makes it a good decision." With this in mind, make sure to follow through on decisions after they are made. Don't waste the time and energy you put into debating the decision by failing to follow through. Also avoid becoming known as the person who dreams big but never acts on their grand plans.

TAKING RISKS

Politician Robert F. Kennedy once said, "Only those who dare to fail greatly can ever achieve greatly." Risk takers such as Kennedy are beloved in American culture and have captured the nation's attention precisely because they were willing to take risks. Most movies, television shows, books, and folklore feature risk takers we admire and aspire to be like. This is because we are not comfortable taking risks, and for good reason. To risk, by definition, includes the potential to fail. Many prefer to play it safe and avoid loss, embarrassment, or a broken heart. But for those who expose themselves to possible danger and, in the end, prevail — that is to be admired.

So, when did we become afraid of trying? Studies show that adolescence is when most people begin to fear taking risks. As children, we are asked to take risks all the time. Every day is a new situation with myriad learning opportunities. We try things, we fall down, we get back up — it is only with time that we learn to avoid falling in the first place. It is important to reawaken the part of you that once knew how to take risks. Recapture that spirit by jumping into the unknown and challenging yourself. When the end result is personal growth, success, and wealth, isn't it worth the risk?

While it's always a good idea to weigh risks and rewards, sometimes you may just have to turn off your brain and act. This is nearly impossible for most of us to do and especially applies to those of us who are chronically indecisive. According to a recent poll, fear of making the wrong decision was second only to fear of failure when asked what prevented people from taking risks. You may have to force yourself to get over the hump by acting without another thought. As Pulitzer Prize-winning author Annie Dillard wrote, "If we listened to our intellect, we'd never have a love affair. We'd never have a friendship. We'd never go into business, because we'd be too cynical. Well, that's nonsense. You've got to jump off cliffs all the time and build your wings on the way down."

An easy way to discern if it is time for you to take a risk is if you are comfortable. Being too comfortable in your ways and means will kill ambition quicker than you can say "risk." As another wise Kennedy, President John F. Kennedy, said, "There are risks and costs to action. But they are far less than the long-range risks of comfortable inaction." When you find yourself filled with fear and unable to invest, buy a home, or try a new romance, consider that the biggest regrets you may ever have are regrets over the things you didn't do. To this end, use the following principles to guide you through the challenges and rewards of responsible risk taking.

PRINCIPLE #142

Discover something new by going first.

Takings risks often requires that you do something that has never been done before. On May 5, 1961, Alan Shepard became the first American to travel to space. His flight aboard the Freedom 7 spacecraft lasted just 15 minutes, but he made history within that short amount of time. Shepard went on to pilot Apollo 14 in 1971 and was the first person to play golf on the moon. Shepard has said, "I think all of us certainly believed the statistics which said that probably 88 percent chance of mission success and maybe 96 percent chance of survival. And we were willing to take those odds."

Principle #143

Leap without looking.

— ✳ —

To take risks, you needn't have every step figured out. In fact, sometimes the best plan is to leap without looking. Millionaires avoid getting bogged down in the details. While they are prepared for certain emergencies, they are also comfortable winging it. When you cruise without a plan, you allow yourself to be more creative and discover ideas you might have missed had you mapped out your whole route. You might be surprised to see how unplanned, time-pressured opportunities unlock your creative and innovative side.

Principle #144

View failure as an opportunity.

Former quarterback Jim McMahon put it best when he said, "Yes, risk-taking is inherently failure-prone. Otherwise, it would be called sure-thing-taking." Of course, the entire reason why something is considered a risk is because you cannot predict what will happen. It's true, the outcome might be failure. The upside to failure, however, is that you always learn something in the process. Demystify failure. Realize it is no big deal to mess up and try again. Once you become unafraid of failure, it won't hold you back from taking risks that are bound to end up successful.

Principle #145

Take courage.

---- ❋ ----

So many of us are afraid to look foolish that we never step outside of our circle of comfort. This type of inactivity is directly linked to our ego. As Elbert Hubbard once said, "The greatest mistake you can make in life is to be continually fearing you will make one." Now is a great time to put yourself out there. Keep in mind that 9 times out of 10, people are not even paying attention to what anyone else is doing anyway. So, don't limit yourself by self-consciousness.

Principle #146

Take risks you can grow into.

———————————— ✳ ————————————

Make the most of every opportunity by creating large parameters that anticipate future growth, not simply ones that meet current needs. If you only plan for what you need today, you will hit the ceiling and have nowhere to grow tomorrow. For example, if you plan to go into business for yourself, keep in mind the growth you anticipate over the next 10 to 15 years. Even if you do not have a staff now, plan to have several employees in the future. Prepare for a much higher income bracket than you currently fit into. Think of your new endeavor as a goldfish — it will grow as big as the bowl you put it in.

Principle #147

Invest as much money as you can afford.

To become a millionaire, you must be prepared to invest. Sadly, the majority of Americans view investing as a dangerous risk. The *Milwaukee Journal Sentinel* found that 44 percent avoid risky investments even if they mean higher returns; 32 percent would feel very insecure if their investments lost as little as 2 percent; and an amazing 56 percent refrain from investing out of fear of risk. Investing is absolutely a risk you will need to take to become a millionaire. To minimize the risk, consult a financial advisor, diversify your portfolio, and educate yourself on stock market trends. You cannot afford to miss out on this integral part of becoming a millionaire.

Principle #148

Recognize that intelligent people take risks.

Though some may call you crazy or even stupid for taking risks, take comfort in knowing that risk taking is a quality that goes hand in hand with being intelligent. In fact, a 2005 study undertaken at the Sloan School of Management at MIT that studied patterns of risk taking in both men and women found that risk takers were likely to have higher IQs than non-risk takers. So don't be afraid to take risks — consider it a sign of your intelligence.

PRINCIPLE #149

Take responsible risks.

※

Never engage in risks that will physically, emotionally, or financially harm you or another person. This does not mean avoid skydiving or rock climbing — these are calculated-risk sports in which risk is reduced through skill and training. Likewise, with proper knowledge, investing in the stock or housing market can be considered calculated risks. Do avoid those risks in which you are sure to gain nothing, lose everything, and put yourself and those around you in danger. Drinking and driving is an unacceptable risk, as is gambling excessively, quitting your job without a plan, and leaving important and potentially lucrative projects until the last minute.

Principle #150

Get rich from taking risks.

—— ✳ ——

The bottom line is that no millionaire ever amassed his or her fortune without taking risks. This is because risks are the only path to the biggest rewards. As author Frank Scully simply put it, "Why not go out on a limb? Isn't that where the fruit is?" To make your first million, you are going to have to take risks, so be willing. They are the only things standing between you and vast rewards.

Overcoming Fear

We are all born fearless and learn how and what to fear as we grow up. Of course, fear is natural and necessary in certain instances. Fear activates our fight-or-flight response — this is the response that will get us out of a burning building or allow us to fight off an attacker. But when fear prevents us from fulfilling our dreams and goals, it must be brought under control. If you intend to become a millionaire you are going to have to do just that.

Fear makes it impossible to put risky plans into effect or embark on new business opportunities that could lead to wealth. In fact, fear may be the aspiring millionaire's greatest obstacle. Fear left unchecked leads to inaction. In other words, if you allow fear to control your life, you will become complacent and sedentary in order to remain safe and avoid risk. But too many of us live our lives avoiding what we are afraid of instead of confronting it. Millionaires never avoid what they fear — they control it and turn it into something that fuels rather than scares them.

One way to gain control over fear is to arm yourself with information. Educate yourself about your fears to expose the myths and realities that surround what scares you. Nine times out of 10 you will find that the danger or risk associated with the fear is exaggerated. For instance, if you feel you deserve a raise but don't ask for one because you are afraid that your boss will laugh at, ridicule, or even fire you, do your homework to assess whether this fear is really founded. Research salary standards online to see if you are being paid above, below, or at national averages for your field. Read studies and statistics on the process of getting a raise. For example, the authors of *Women Don't Ask: Negotiation and the Gender Divide* say that women tend to underestimate the amount of money available for raises and salary and thus typically ask for and get less than men — on average, 30 percent less. After arming yourself with information about raises, you will realize that worrying your boss will fire or ridicule you was a waste of time. In fact, the worst he or she will probably say is a simple, "I'm sorry, it's not in the budget. Let's revisit the topic in 6 months."

Inspirational author and self-help guru Anthony Robbins has written, "Do what you fear, and the death of fear is certain." It is true that the only way to conquer a fear is to confront it head on and then leave it behind. The following principles will provide you with the tools to help you identify and face the fears that stand in your way of becoming a millionaire.

PRINCIPLE #151

Educate yourself away from fear.

———————————— ❋ ————————————

Fear is the number one reason people do not become millionaires. One study found that 80 to 85 percent of Americans do not invest their money because they are afraid to lose it. Investing is a risky endeavor, but there are ways to make sound decisions and your investments sure things over time. Too many people have given up the chance to be millionaires simply because they were afraid to learn about the realities of investing. Educate yourself about investing by taking a class on the stock market or joining an investment group.

PRINCIPLE #152

Let the great unknown become an adventure.

Uncertainty does not have to equal fear. It is exciting to not always know what comes next. Allow your mind to go with the flow and be open to discoveries that come with exploring uncharted territory. For example, imagine the fear Lewis and Clark must have felt when Thomas Jefferson sent them west to find a water route to the Pacific Ocean. If they'd refused the assignment based on fear of the unknown, they never would have gone down in history as 2 of the world's greatest explorers.

Principle #153

Tune out fear mongers.

Everyone knows that person who tries to scare you to death over a simple decision or idea. This person is afraid to change and grow, so he or she tries to keep everyone else from moving forward. If you are to become a millionaire you must tune out people who do not support your endeavors. Recognize that such people are afraid to let you surpass them. Never internalize their fears as your own. In fact, there may come a time when you must cut such people out of your life as it becomes clear they do not wish the best for you.

PRINCIPLE #154

Disconnect from anxiety by engaging only in positive self-talk.

───────── ✳ ─────────

Negative self-talk fuels your anxiety and leads to diminished self-esteem. The state that you put yourself in after hours of "I can't" will prevent you from ever becoming a millionaire. Positive self-talk has been scientifically proven to improve performance; according to a reputable psychological study of gymnasts, the number one fear of competitive gymnasts is injury during a routine. The study found that gymnasts who engaged in positive self-talk before practices and meets were significantly less likely to be injured than those who did not. Avoid injuring your chances of becoming a millionaire by engaging only in positive self-talk.

Principle #155

Find others who share your goals but not your fears.

Seek out others who share your drive to become a millionaire. Working in harmony with a group of like-minded individuals can create what Napoleon Hill calls the "master mind." This idea supposes that when a group of people comes together with the same goal, their ideas create a positive energy that is accessible to everyone. This is also true of fear. If you surround yourself with naysayers and fearful people, your group's energy will be about fear, not success.

Principle #156

Confront your fears one step at a time.

---　✳　---

Fear is insidious and will crush your dreams if left unchecked. One way to halt the demolition of your goals is to confront your fear one small step at a time. For example, if you are afraid of dogs, start spending some time at a local pet shelter. You will be protected from the dogs by cages but still able to interact with them. Next, try holding a puppy and work your way up in age and size. Do the same with becoming a millionaire. Become comfortable with investing by opening a Certificate of Deposit. Next, take a course on playing the stock market.

Principle #157

Don't exaggerate threat levels.

In the age of the war on terror, we are repeatedly told to be on high alert. Absorbing this message leads us to become fearful that at any moment, our world may crumble. However, odds are slim that the threats you fear are realistic. Exaggerating threat levels is a surefire way to miss opportunities that can help you become a millionaire. For instance, if you are afraid of flying, you're likely to avoid business opportunities that require travel. But the National Transportation Safety Board says the odds of being killed in a plane crash are 52.6 million to 1. Always find out how realistic a threat is before being dissuaded from your goal.

Principle #158

Turn fear into challenge.

Writer Henry S. Haskins thought to turn fear around in the following way: "Panic at the thought of doing a thing is a challenge to do it." Turn your greatest fear on its head by confronting it. If you fear investing (as do 56 percent of Americans, according to the *Milwaukee Journal Sentinel*), purposefully sign up for an investment class to explain the process for you. If you fear the dentist (as do 58 percent of Americans), schedule an appointment with your dentist to have him or her explain what goes on during a check-up. Confronting your fears will demystify them, allowing them to be conquered.

Principle #159

Always be prepared.

The best way to alleviate anxiety is to be prepared. For example, if you are afraid of public speaking (consistently ranked as the number one fear of Americans), do more research than is required on the subject you are presenting. Feeling confident about the material will alleviate your fear of public speaking. Also, map out your route and drive to the venue at least once before the day you are scheduled to speak. In addition, try to find out as much as you can about your audience so that you have friendly and appropriate anecdotes ready. Preparing is a surefire way to dissolve the fear of doing something outside of your comfort zone.

Keeping the Faith

Much of what happens in the world is impossible for us to understand. Yet, as humans we try our best to make sense of seemingly incomprehensible events such as violence, greed, and war. When we witness such horrors, many of us are tempted to turn away from our faith because it has failed to explain why bad things happen to good people. Indeed, all the major religions have focused much of their creeds on attempting to answer this question, which in religious circles is known as *theodicy*.

Turning away from faith never serves the greater good in your life. Having faith, it has been argued by theologians, is necessary to know anything at all. Saint Augustine once said, "Believe in order that you may understand." In other words, one must assume, believe, or have faith before one can acquire knowledge. Therefore, it is wise to have faith in something outside of yourself — in God, the universe, or karma — to operate as a guiding force in your life.

Faith need not be practiced through an organized religion. In fact, those who cull the tenets from many religions they find most appealing are more likely to have a stronger connection to their higher power. Having faith allows you to relax the reins a little bit and trust that the universe wants what is best for you. Of course, you do have responsibility to act in kindness and with good intentions to expect these things in return. But with faith to guide you, along with the following simple principles, practicing kindness, patience, and gratitude will become second nature in no time.

Principle #160

Have faith in a higher power.

It is normal to experience periods of doubt and confusion at times, especially when embarking on something as challenging as becoming a millionaire. But when you find yourself in a place where your faith falters, don't let it go. Studies show time and again that people who have faith in a higher power recover faster from surgeries and are better equipped to deal with emotional upheaval. As the director of the inspirational classic film *Miracle on 34th Street*, George Seaton, once said, "Faith is believing in things when common sense tells you not to."

Principle #161

Assume that good faith abounds.

We all make assumptions about things we are unsure of. So, why not use assumption to your benefit? Assume that the universe will give you what you want. It does nothing for you to expect to be thwarted. Learn to extend the assumption of good faith to everyone you meet. Treating others as if they intend only goodness will bring out their best qualities. Whereas, assuming the worst in others will likely have them meet your expectations.

Principle #162

Know that the universe will reward your courage to realize your goals.

People of courage are rewarded in many ways. Some rewards are internal — personal satisfaction, growth, and pride. Most of us also want external recognition for our courage, too. This is where you must have faith that the universe is paying attention and will reward your courageous efforts to achieve your goals. Rhonda Byrne, author of the best-selling book *The Secret*, writes that the universe will give you what you ask for if you attract it by making your desires known. Rest assured that courageously seeking your goals is most definitely letting the universe know what you are after.

Principle #163

Have faith that God wants you to succeed.

It is wonderful to discover that God wants the very best for you. This comes from having faith that God wants you to succeed — and really believing it. To truly become a faithful person, you must avoid approaching faith from a guilty place. Don't try to force faith because your family or religion tells you to believe. Instead, make your faith personal. Decide for yourself the things in which you most believe and stick with them. People who come to faith on their own terms report a deeper connection to God and overall sense of well-being.

Principle #164

Trust that even though you cannot see the end result, it's coming.

It is a great challenge for most of us to believe in what we cannot see or immediately know. But it is important to trust that though you cannot yet see the end result of your efforts toward wealth, millionaire status is coming if you truly want it badly enough. In fact, most great journeys begin with someone trusting in a certain outcome. For example, chemist Michael Polanyi once suggested that scientific analysis starts with faith that discovering something new is possible. Trusting that your desired outcome is on the horizon is a necessary part of making it so.

PRINCIPLE #165

Let faith trump reality.

━━━━━━━━━━━━━━ ❋ ━━━━━━━━━━━━━━

Sometimes it helps our sense of well-being to disregard reality and coast for awhile on faith. For instance, victims of Hurricane Katrina reported that what kept them going in the midst of losing their loved ones, their homes, and having to live without running water or electricity was their faith that the horrible reality was temporary and would not last. When you find yourself in a situation you would never choose for yourself, let faith take the reins and guide you to a more pleasant tomorrow. Always keep in mind this truism: "This, too, shall pass."

Principle #166

Realize that no one is doomed to bad luck.

Relinquish any idea that you are a victim of bad luck. Luck refers to random, circumstantial occurrences that are beyond your control. Therefore, it does not make sense to say you are on the receiving end of luck, good or bad. Instead of blaming luck for your circumstance, take a realistic look at your mindset and efforts at change. Take the time to articulate goals and then being working toward them. Keep in mind that people who believe they are doomed to bad luck are looking for an excuse to fail.

Principle #167

Believe that your goals serve a purpose.

There is no greater threat to success than losing faith that your goals serve a purpose. This frequently happens after a period of time where you have felt stagnant. During such moments, you should revisit the reasons why you decided to become a millionaire in the first place. When you write down a goal, write why you want to achieve it and what purpose it will serve. Doing so will help remind you that you once believed in what you were doing and where you were headed. Detailed records are an invaluable tool for keeping yourself on track when you lose your way.

Principle #168

Trust in a grand plan to stay motivated.

— ✳ —

Martin Luther King Jr. once said, "Faith is taking the first step even when you don't see the whole staircase." Indeed, putting your trust in the existence of a grand plan is difficult at times, but important. Humans have an inherent need to organize chaos. The way to do that when it comes to life, death, tragedy, and joy is to believe in a grand plan that is the destination to which all individual lives lead. Finding meaning through believing in the grand plan will help alleviate spiritual crises and bring joy, meaning, and purpose to your life.

SAVING MONEY

Contrary to popular belief, there is very little mystery to how to save money. In fact, it really is as simple as spend less money than you bring in — and save what's left over. Yet, most Americans under the age of 35 have a net worth of just $14,200. If these folks were forced to retire today, they'd be in severe trouble. Increasing your net worth and controlling your spending, however, will put you on the fast track toward accumulating wealth.

There are many ways to decrease your monthly spending, and chief among them is to cut credit-card debt out of your life. Indeed, credit-card debt is probably the worst type of debt to incur. This is because interest rates often end up somewhere between 13 and 20 percent and sometimes range as high as 39.99 percent, if you have late payments or other penalties on your account. High interest rates lead to a fantastic waste of money. If you owed $1,000 on a credit card that had a 21 percent interest rate, you would pay more than $200 per year in interest. That's $200 you could otherwise put toward savings.

One of the best ways to decrease your spending is to cut up your credit cards and only use cash and debit cards. Relying on cash alone, rather than credit, will ensure you are not spending more than you have. You will also likely think harder before purchasing items — studies have shown that people are more reluctant to make purchases with cash because the fact that they are spending their hard-earned money is more apparent to them. Reducing your reliance on credit cards is just one lifestyle change you can make to save money. Factor in this and the following principles for saving as you embark on the path to wealth.

Principle #169

Pay off credit card debt.

Eliminating credit-card debt is the very first step you must take to become a millionaire. Even if you opened your credit-card account with 0 percent interest, chances are that rate will skyrocket when the introductory offer expires. You can expect to be charged from 13 to 39.99 percent interest on your balance. The average American household has at least $8,000 in credit-card debt and pays an average of 15 percent interest on it. Do not become another American who throws money away on credit cards for the privilege of making everyday purchases. Get out of credit-card debt as fast as you possibly can.

Principle #170

Open a savings account today.

— ✳ —

There are several types of savings accounts available, and you should choose one that best suits your needs. If you have money that can sit for awhile, a Certificate of Deposit (CD) may be a good choice. CDs are deposits that you promise not to touch for a certain amount of time. In exchange for leaving the funds with the financial institution, you receive a higher interest rate on your deposit. However, if you need to access your account in a hurry, an instant-access savings account may be more suitable. These accounts pay lower interest rates but are good for setting aside emergency money.

Principle #171

Track your spending habits.

---------------------------------- ❋ ----------------------------------

To save money, you must pay attention to where you spend it. Account for every penny that leaves your wallet. Set aside a container in which to store receipts. Each time you purchase something — anything from a newspaper to an expensive gift — put the receipt in the box. Once a month, add up all of the receipts and compare the total to your pay stubs for the month. This process is enlightening and can be quite shocking. Most people have no idea that their morning latté adds up to more than $60 per month or that their fast-food lunch totals more than $120 each month.

Principle #172

Get out of the red and into the black.

About 43 percent of American families spend more money than they bring in annually. This means every month they are in the red. If you are part of this group, you must start bringing in more money than you spend. One way to do this is to increase your income. Ask for a raise, get a part-time job, or sell some old possessions on eBay. If you cannot increase your income, you must reduce your spending. To get back in the black, get spending under control by eating fewer meals out and shopping less.

PRINCIPLE #173

Control the urge to splurge.

—— ❋ ——

There is no greater threat to your savings than emotional spending. Far too many of us indulge in "retail therapy" when we are feeling depressed, bored, or out of control. Shopping to alter your mood is tempting because it provides instant gratification. But if you truly want to become a millionaire, you must realize that emotional spending hurts your goal. Think of all the items in your house that, if you could, you would return for a full refund. You would likely have thousands of extra dollars. The next time you are overcome by the urge to splurge, resist it with all your might.

Principle #174

Use cash whenever possible.

Credit-card debt in America has gone up 167 percent since 1990. This is because people use credit cards to live beyond their means. Financial experts agree that to reduce debt you should only purchase that which you have the cash to buy. This will require some sacrifice on your part, but the end result will be worth it: more cash in your pocket and less handed over to the credit collectors.

PRINCIPLE #175

Establish an emergency fund.

❈

To secure your wealth, it is a good idea to build up a financial reserve. You should have enough money saved to pay for 3 to 6 months' worth of living expenses. This way you are not forced to sustain yourself by taking out a loan against your house or to subsist on credit cards. Work hard to establish a "nest egg" that is constantly nurtured. Never tap into it except when you are hit with an emergency, such as losing your job, becoming ill, or another tragedy that deals a blow to your income.

Principle #176

Make a budget.

Often, people avoid making a budget for themselves because it feels restrictive or limiting. But spending without a plan is a recipe for financial ruin. You must create a budget and respect its boundaries. See boundaries not as limits but as guides toward wealth. Imagine that you are creating what financial expert Loral Langemeier calls the "wealth cycle process." This concept has you focus on what you can do with the money you have instead of what you cannot do. Spending your money with purpose and intention is the responsible way to stay out of debt and amass wealth.

Principle #177

 Realize that imaginary
money doesn't count.

——————————— ✳ ———————————

A famous scene from *National Lampoon's Christmas Vacation* occurs when Clark W. Griswold unveils his present to the family — a swimming pool! Clark puts a down payment on the pool, banking that his Christmas bonus will cover the rest. But, that bonus never comes — instead, Clark's boss enrolls him in a jelly-of-the-month club. Like Clark, many of us spend against money we do not yet have, such as annual bonuses, inheritances, dividends, and holiday gifts. Avoid this trap by only spending money you can literally see.

Principle #178

Save money by changing your habits at home.

— ❋ —

You don't have to overhaul your lifestyle to save money. Simple steps you take today will help you cut spending in your own home. Immediate cost reductions include unplugging power adapters when not in use, washing your clothes in cold water, and remembering to turn off the lights when you leave a room. Additionally, make sure your refrigerator is up to date. Older refrigerators cost at least an extra $125 per year to run. Next, change all of the light bulbs in your house. Fluorescent bulbs consume 4 times less energy than incandescent bulbs and last 8 times as long.

Principle #179

There is no amount too small to save.

Many of us refrain from saving $100 here and there because it seems like too small an amount to really influence our financial future. We think, "What's the point of denying myself this nice meal, new sweater, or upgraded iPod? It's not like an extra $200 is going to make me a millionaire." But even if you only increase your income by $200 each month, in 25 years, given an 8 percent return on your money and an average inflation rate of 3.1 percent, you will save an additional $72,000 which, in 25 years, will actually be worth about $100,000. So never underestimate the power of each saved dollar.

INVESTING YOUR MONEY

Business tycoon and author of the best-selling book *The One Minute Millionaire*, Robert G. Allen, has remarked, "How many millionaires do you know who have become wealthy by investing in savings accounts? I rest my case." Indeed, it will be impossible for you to become a millionaire unless you become comfortable investing your money in the stock market, real estate, business ventures, and other money-making vehicles.

Before you decide how to invest, you must be clear on what you want your money to do. Articulate how you plan to spend the money eventually — this will help you determine what type of investment to make with it. If you want to accrue a down payment for a house you plan to buy in 5 years, you can feel comfortable tying your money up in an account you cannot immediately access. If you want to accrue enough money to fund 3 to 6 months of living expenses should you become unemployed or incapacitated, you will want to invest in something more liquid, for easy access to your money at any time. The general rule with investing is that you pay a premium for having access to your money; accounts that you can access immediately pay lower interest than accounts you cannot. Articulating what you plan to use your invested money for will help you determine what types of investments to make.

Investing in stock is no doubt the most lucrative choice. There are a plethora of stocks and quite a few markets in which you can invest. Do your homework and make selections that best suit your goals. Keep in mind that historically, the annual rate of return for stocks is around 10 percent. Thus, if you invested $10,000, you would see a dividend of $1,000. But there is always risk in playing the market, and profits are never guaranteed. Make sure to educate yourself before making any investments. You can check a company's credit-worthiness by visiting www.standardandpoors.com or www.moodys.com. Should you hit a wall, don't be afraid to enlist the skills of a financial analyst. The fact is it would take volumes to cover everything there is to know about investing. But the following simple principles will get you well on your way to becoming a millionaire through your investments.

Principle #180

Avoid "get rich quick" scams.

———————— ✳ ————————

Be aware of schemes that promise to solve your financial problems or scams that swear to make you thousands each month. There is a huge industry devoted to ripping you off, and the less savvy among us have become its victim and lost entire savings in the meantime. Beware of any program, person, or pitch that sounds too good to be true or even illegal. Becoming comfortable with simple financial concepts is one way to avoid being preyed upon by schemers.

Principle #181

Buy a house.

Owning a home is literally putting money in the bank. Owning a home creates equity. Your equity is the difference between the market value of your home and the outstanding loan balance. The less you owe on a home, the more equity you have. Consider too that the cost of renting is expected to reach mortgage levels within the next 10 to 15 years. If the monthly costs of renting and owning become the same, wouldn't you feel better knowing your money is going toward your own equity instead of your landlord's?

Principle #182

Find out if your company offers an
Employee Stock Purchase Plan (ESPP).

An excellent way to save on stocks and get practice investing is to buy stock through your job. Many publicly traded companies offer their employees the opportunity to buy company stock at a discount to its fair market value. This means you can buy shares in the company for less money than if you were a broker. By purchasing stock at a bargain, you can save as much as 15 percent. Also, you are not required to report this as income until you sell the stock. Finally, employers make it simple by deducting the fee from your paycheck.

Principle #183

Purchase stock.

Most (if not all) people of wealth have a significant investment portfolio that includes stocks. Having stock means that you have partial ownership in a publicly traded company. "Publicly traded" simply means ownership has been divided up into "shares." When you purchase stock, you become a shareholder in the company. The more money you invest in stocks, the higher your dividend (quarterly payout of profits) will be. Another way to earn money from stocks is to sell your shares when prices are high.

PRINCIPLE #184

Let a professional manage your investments until you know what you are doing.

Though it is possible to learn how to become a savvy investor, it can be daunting and time consuming. In this case, consider hiring a professional investment manager or advisor. These professionals are paid to study market trends and to assess risks. Your investments will be given full-time attention, and you will spend less time worrying about managing your own accounts. Investment management companies will have several portfolios to choose from based on your financial situation and will be available to respond to your questions and concerns.

Principle #185

Invest in a mutual fund.

———————————— ❈ ————————————

Mutual funds are like a large investment club composed of people who pool their money together to make a variety of investments. A full-time investment manager is in charge of buying and selling the various stocks, so there is little effort on your part. The manager has a high stake in the success of your portfolio, because his salary is tied to how well your investments are doing. Buying mutual funds is relatively inexpensive — as little as $1,000 can get you in. Mutual funds are considered to be on the safer side of investing since the protective Investment Company Act was passed in 1940.

Principle #186

Invest more money and receive a higher yield.

It is important to invest as much money as you can afford. Of course, you should never invest money that will compromise savings, or so much money that you cannot keep up your standard of living. But once you decide how much money you can afford to invest, don't be squeamish about using it. Keep in mind that a $1,000 investment will reap 10 times more revenue than a $100 investment. So to see your bank accounts rise, play with as large an amount as you can reasonably afford.

PRINCIPLE #187

Establish a baseline for how low your stock may fall.

When investing, always have an exit strategy. It is simply irresponsible to continue past the point of no return. This happens when people fail to pay attention to their portfolio or when they engage in overly risky investing. Don't let your ego rule your investments. If you notice your stock falling, be prepared to act. Predetermine the point that you will sell your stock, should it drop significantly. This is your exit strategy. Next, be ready to sell off your shares once the stock reaches your predetermined low point.

Principle #188

Diversify your investment portfolio.

If ever there was an appropriate application of the advice "don't put all your eggs in one basket," it is investing. Never invest all your funds in one type of company. Furthermore, never invest all your funds in one type of account. Make sure your portfolio reflects the wide range of investment opportunities out there. Choose a blend of high- and low-growth investments to balance each other out. Choose investments in a wide range of markets that will not be affected by one another. Keeping your eggs in many baskets will ensure a well-rounded, strong portfolio.

Principle #189

Be prepared not to see a return on your investment.

Investing your hard-earned money inherently involves risk. Sometimes the risk is minimal and other times the risks can be catastrophic. It is important to know up front that there are no guarantees with investing. There are events beyond your control that can drastically affect the value of your investments. These include natural disasters, terrorist attacks, inflation, and the sometimes-frenzied flux of market value (such as the rise and fall of the dotcoms in the 1990s). Investing is truly a "buyers beware" venture. Don't get involved until you are comfortable with this reality.

Principle #190

Never quit investing once you reach your financial goals.

There truly is no such thing as too much money. When you are done buying everything you have ever dreamed for you and your loved ones, you can use your excess money to create organizations, donate to charity, or fund a politician of your choice. Just as someone who has lost 100 pounds must not renege on the diet and exercise changes they have made in their life, neither should you abandon the lifestyle, mindset, and discipline that allowed you to become a millionaire. So never quit once you reach your financial goals; you will always be able to find something wonderful to do with your money.

PLANNING FOR RETIREMENT

Retirement planning takes years of preparation. This is especially true if you plan to retire as a millionaire. To retire with more money than required to merely get by, start today to educate yourself about the various retirement savings plans and how to make wise investments. Do not allow another minute to go by without setting some financial goals for your golden years. The more time, thought, and action you invest in your retirement fund the more comfortable you will be when it comes time to close your office door for the last time. Indeed, when it comes to saving for your retirement goals, remember that "the sooner the better" always applies.

Planning for your retirement requires that you take steps to ensure your basic needs are met. Savvy investing will put you in the position to live off interest and dividends instead of depending on government subsidies. The sad truth is that we no longer live in a world where we can depend on Social Security benefits to meet our basic needs. In fact, Social Security will only pay between 30 and 40 percent of living expenses. In other words, if you need $1,000 per week to live, you will only receive $300 or $400 from Social Security. As living costs escalate and the threat of diminished Social Security benefits becomes imminent, it is wise to take immediate steps to augment your funds. Luckily, there are many ways to prepare for retirement, and it is never too late to start. In fact, if you follow these simple principles for retirement planning, you can ensure you will be thriving, not just surviving, in your golden years.

Principle #191

Save now, retire early!

It is never too early to begin saving for retirement. It is also never too late, so don't become discouraged if you haven't begun yet. You are not alone: Eighty percent of baby boomers do not have a significant retirement "nest egg." The average baby boomer household has less than $50,000 in savings, which is far from enough money to support the retired lifestyle. Start saving now so that when it comes time for you to retire, you can do so with peace of mind.

PRINCIPLE #192

Never assume someone else has planned for you.

Young people often count on inheriting money to cover their living expenses once they retire. This can be a catastrophic mistake. Chances are your parents (or grandparents) will become engaged in a "reverse mortgage" to supplement their own retirement income. This is when a lender distributes to a homeowner a monthly payment in return for title on the home. Since homeownership makes up the majority of a person's assets, in this case, there would be very little in the way of an inheritance. Don't bank on coming into money. Instead, plan for your own retirement by saving and investing now.

Principle #193

Open an IRA.

Individual Retirement Accounts (IRA) are simply tax-deferred savings accounts. As long as the money remains in the account, earnings are not taxed. The money is then invested in stocks, bonds, mutual funds, and real estate. If you are less than 50 years old, you may contribute up to $4,000 each year, while those 50 and older may contribute $5,000 per year. This means if you are 39 and you put $4,000 annually into an IRA, by the time you are 59 years old (the age at which you may withdraw funds without penalty) you will have a minimum of $80,000 (plus earned interest). Visit www.ira.com for more information.

Principle #194

Switch to a Roth IRA if you are eligible.

— ❋ —

Roth IRAs are similar to traditional IRAs. Like IRAs, you are able to contribute $4,000 if you are less than 50 years old, and if you are 50 years or older you may contribute up to $5,000 per year into the account. The major difference with a Roth IRA is that these accounts are designed for people who anticipate that their income tax rate will be higher at the time of retirement than it is now. Roth IRAs require that you pay taxes up front and then do not pay taxes upon distribution of funds. There are limitations, however. For more information visit www.rothira.com.

PRINCIPLE #195

Invest at least 15 percent of your annual income in a 401(k).

Many companies offer their employees the opportunity to participate in a 401(k) savings plan. 401(k) plans allow you to put pre-tax income into a tax-deferred investment account. A special feature of the plan is that many companies offer a match program. Sometimes they will match 50 percent of your contribution, meaning for every dollar you put in the account, your employer will contribute 50 cents. You can see how quickly this type of savings plan adds up! Financial experts recommend that you contribute at least 15 percent of your annual income to a 401(k) account. For more information visit www.401k.org.

Principle #196

Take your 401(k) with you.

---------- ※ ----------

Once you've established a 401(k) savings plan, don't give it up! You have a few options if you must leave your job. If your new job offers a 401(k), ask to transfer your funds to your new retirement plan. Or, you can roll your account balance into an IRA. Finally, if you have at least $5,000 in your 401(k), you can let the money sit. You will no longer be able to make contributions and your former employer will not contribute to the fund, but this helps people who are unsure of what to do next and want to let the money sit while they figure it out — especially if the account is doing well.

Principle #197

Avoid borrowing against your 401(k).

— ✳ —

Though borrowing against a 401(k) is allowed, it can be very risky business. Investors are allowed to borrow against them for major purchases, such as a home down payment. While this seems tempting, remember, on average, lenders require these loans to be repaid within 15 to 20 years, and in the current economic climate, no job is secure beyond 2 to 4 years. If you take out a loan against your 401(k) and then lose your job, you only have 60 days to repay the loan in full. Don't make the nightmare of having to come up with $50,000 in 60 days your reality.

PRINCIPLE #198

Do not invest all of your 401(k) money in one company.

The best way to maximize your retirement savings is to diversify your investments. Nothing proved this more than the Enron disaster. A very high percentage of Enron employees had the bulk of their 401(k) investments tied up in company stock. When Enron went under, stock prices for the company fell from $90 per share to 30 cents per share. People who invested solely in company stock lost their entire retirement savings accounts. So, when choosing where to put your 401(k), select from a number of companies and types of investments. Have a healthy portfolio that includes stocks, bonds, mutual funds, and real estate investments.

Principle #199

Pay off credit card debt by the time you are within 10 years of retirement.

Credit card debt is America's fastest-growing economic problem. One in 4 American families have reached or exceeded their credit card limits. Most households have at least 2 credit cards, and people within 10 years of retirement age spend ⅓ of their income on debt payments. The toll this way of living takes on retirement is catastrophic. To avoid the devastation of credit card debt, make it a priority to pay off all credit cards by the time you are within 10 years of retirement. This will allow you time to start to build savings and rescue your golden years from the clutches of debt collectors.

Principle #200

Withdraw wisely.

Once you retire, financial experts recommend that you do not withdraw more than 4 or 5 percent of your nest egg each year. You want to manage your money in such a way that you pay the least amount of taxes possible. Remember, each time you make a withdrawal from a retirement account you must pay taxes on the distributed funds. However, leaving the bulk of your savings in 401(k) and IRA plans allows interest to continue to accrue, without having to pay taxes. This also increases the likelihood that you will outlive your assets, which is an important goal for retirees.

Additional Information and Ideas

The following pages contain a few exercises that will help you achieve your goal of becoming a millionaire. The more you practice these exercises, the more your chances of attaining wealth will improve.

Make a habit of performing these exercises whenever you are feeling derailed or discouraged. These exercises will help you overcome obstacles that are preventing you from becoming a millionaire. They will also help you get back on track with your financial goals.

Practice these exercises so you can increase your income, become comfortable with financial terms and concepts, and learn the basics of investing. Each of these skills must be mastered if you are to become a millionaire.

These exercises will put you on the fast track to becoming a millionaire in the following ways:

Tips for Increasing Your Income
Whether it be starting a side business or asking for a raise, there are ways you can start earning more money today.

Investing Money
This exercise presents you with some investing basics and points you toward sources of further learning.

Basic Investment Terms
Becoming comfortable with financial terms is essential to becoming a millionaire.

Tips for Increasing Your Income

Start a small side business.
What hobbies do you have that can be turned into a lucrative opportunity? Most hobbies can easily be turned into extra income. Consider selling your items on eBay or on Craigslist. Or ask local retailers to stock your one-of-a-kind creations.

Earn an advanced degree.
Consider that the average net worth of someone with a college degree is $226,100. Net worth only goes up from there. So, invest in an advanced degree. Check to see if your company has a tuition reimbursement program or if you can take night courses at a local university.

Ask for a raise.
Check The Bureau of Labor Statistics (www.bls.gov/ncs/) to see if you are earning a competitive wage. If not, ask for a raise. Explain your value to the company and have plans ready for improvements. Be prepared to negotiate!

Ask for extra work and get paid for it.
Write up a proposal to do extra work — and get paid for it. Give your boss a detailed descriptions of how you plan to manage your job and additional work. You'll need to demonstrate it is the only way to get extra projects done.

Generate more clients for your current business.
Invest extra money to advertise your services. Seek out inexpensive but high-profile advertising spaces, such as on bus benches or T-shirts. Also, send monthly mailings with information about your services and contact information to everyone in your address book.

Raise your fees.
Every 2 years, it is acceptable to raise your fees slightly to reflect the cost of living. To offset the ruffled feathers of regular customers, be sure to give them ample notice and offer 1 free use of your services.

INVESTING MONEY

When you decide to invest your hard-earned money you may feel overwhelmed by all there is to know. One of the first important concepts to learn is that of "risk and return." Risk and return means that the payments you will receive on your principle will vary. Keep in mind that you may even lose your initial investment. However, even if you do nothing with your money but spend and save, you risk not having enough of it to buy a house or to retire. Deciding to take a chance on investing is a risk that may reap major financial rewards. The thing to remember with risk and return is that if you a take a more expensive risk, you may expect to get greater returns. So, how much risk are you willing to take with your money? The answer depends on factors such as your age, income, and financial goals. No matter where you invest your money, it is your responsibility to first become an educated investor.

The following websites can help you with your research:

BusinessWeek Online: An award-winning site where you can find in-depth stock and investing news and articles; the online supplement to *BusinessWeek* magazine (www. businessweekonline).

Charles Schwab: An investment company. The website (www.schwab.com) provides ample free information for both new and seasoned investors.

Dow Jones & Company: Publishes business and financial news and information (www.dj.com).

Edustock: An educational web page (http://library.thinkquest. org/3088/) that teaches how the stock market works. It includes tutorials and a free 20-minute stock market simulation.

401(k).org: A public service to help individuals learn about saving and investing for retirement. This site (www.401k. org) is maintained by the Profit Sharing/401(k) Council of America.

Morningstar.com: Retirement planning and investment tools and calculators (www.morningstar.com).

NASDAQ: National Association of Securities Dealers Automated Quotations system website (www.nasdaq.com/ aspx/iishome.aspx). Its list includes approximately 3,200 companies and, on average, trades more shares per day than any other U.S. market.

NYSE: New York Stock Exchange website (www.nyse.com).

Optima Investment: Comprehensive daily research on the world's financial markets, including economic news and analysis, a global financial calendar with market expectations, technical analysis commentary and support resistance levels, and tables with technical indicators and volatility statistics (www.optimainvestor.com).

Roth IRA: Provides technical and planning information on Roth IRAs (an individual retirement account) to practitioners and consumers (www.rothira.com).

T. Rowe Price: A company that offers investment guidance and advice for individual investors (www.troweprice.com).

TheStreet.com: A timely commentary on stock market news, stock picks, investment advice, and quotes (www.thestreet.com).

Basic Investment Terms

Here are some important, useful investment terms:

A-D: Advance-Decline, or measurement of the number of issues trading above their previous closing prices less the number trading below their previous closing prices over a particular period. As a technical measure of market breadth, the steepness of the A-D line indicates whether a strong bull or bear market is under way.

ASSETS: Resources owned by a company, fund, or individual. Some examples are cash, investments, money due, materials, and inventories.

BALANCE SHEET: A formal statement of assets, liabilities, and equity as of a specific date.

BEAR MARKET: A market in which securities or commodities are persistently declining in value. A "bear" will reference an individual who will sell in anticipation of a price decline.

BOND: A debt security issued by corporations, governments, or their agencies, in return for cash from lenders and investors. A bond holder is not a shareholder but a creditor.

BULL MARKET: A market in which securities or commodities are persistently rising in value.

BURN RATE: The rate (usually calculated monthly) at which a new company or venture spends its capital before it starts to realize profits.

COMMODITY: A tradable item that can generally be further processed and sold; examples include gold, corn, wheat, natural gas, and oil.

COMPOUND INTEREST: Interest that is calculated on both the principal and interest previously earned.

DIVIDEND: The amount of a corporation's after-tax earnings that it pays to its shareholders.

DOW JONES INDEX: A leading index of U.S. stock market prices.

EQUITY: Ownership interest in a company in the form of common or preferred stock. This is the risk-bearing portion of the firm's capital in contrast to its debt capital, which is usually secured by assets. Creditors take priority over shareholders should the company become insolvent and its assets distributed.

FINANCIAL ANALYST: A professional that advises clients on the likelihood of risk and return of investments; one who manages investment portfolios.

GLAMOUR STOCK: A popular stock characterized by high earnings growth rate and a price that rise is faster than the market average in a bull market.

INDEPENDENT BROKER: Member on the floor of the NYSE who executes orders for other brokers having more business at that time than they can handle themselves, or for firms who do not have their exchange member on the floor.

INVESTMENT: An asset acquired for the purpose of producing income and/or capital gains.

INVESTMENT BANKER: Also known as an underwriter. The middleman between the corporation issuing new securities and the public. The usual practice is for one or more investment bankers to buy outright from a corporation a new issue of stocks or bonds. The group forms a syndicate to sell the securities to individuals and institutions. Investment bankers also distribute very large blocks of stocks or bonds — perhaps held by an estate.

LIQUIDITY: The ability of an investment to be easily converted into cash with little or no loss or delay.

MARKET: A public place where buyers and sellers conduct transactions, either directly or via intermediaries.

MUTUAL FUND: A form of collective investments that pools money from many investors and puts their money in stocks, bonds, short-term money market instruments, and other securities.

NATIONAL ASSOCIATION OF SECURITIES DEALERS AUTOMATED QUOTATIONS (NASDAQ): The New York-based U.S. stock exchange that specializes in technology companies.

PORTFOLIO: An investor's collection of investment holdings. A diverse portfolio refers to a collection of stocks culled from different industries and that reflect different levels of risk.

PREFERRED STOCK: A class of ownership in a company, with a stated dividend that is paid before dividends to common stockholders. Preferred shares rarely hold voting rights. Preferred shareholders have priority over common stockholders on earnings and assets in the event of liquidation, after creditors are repaid.

PRIVATE EQUITY: Shares in a company that are available to investors but are not quoted on a stock market. Companies often use these funds to develop new products, expand working capital, make acquisitions, or strengthen the balance sheet.

PROSPECTUS: A legal document, required by the Securities Act of 1933, setting forth the complete history and current status of a security or fund; it must be made available whenever an offer to sell is made to the public.

QUOTE: The highest bid to buy and the lowest offer to sell a security in a given market at a given time. If you ask your financial advisor for a "quote" on a stock, he or she may come back with something like "45 1/4 to 45 1/2." This means that $45.25 is the highest price any buyer wanted to pay at the time the quote was given and that $45.50 was the lowest price that any seller would take at the same time.

RED HERRING: A registration statement filed with but not yet approved by the Securities and Exchange Commission (SEC).

RETURN: The change in the value of a portfolio over an evaluation period, including any distributions made from the portfolio during that period.

SECURITIES AND EXCHANGE COMMISSION (SEC): A federal agency that regulates the U.S. financial markets. The SEC also oversees the securities industry and promotes full disclosure in order to protect the investing public against malpractice in the securities markets.

SELLING ON THE GOOD NEWS: A strategy of selling stock shortly after a company announces good news and the stock price rises. Investors believe that the price is as high as it can go and is on the brink of going down.

SIMPLE INTEREST: Interest that is paid on the initial investment alone.

STOCK: An instrument that signifies an ownership position (equity) in a corporation.

STOCK DIVIDEND: A dividend paid in securities rather than in cash. The dividend may be additional shares of the issuing company, or in shares of another company (usually a subsidiary) held by the company.

VENTURE CAPITAL: An investment in a start-up business that is perceived to have excellent growth prospects but does not have access to capital markets. Type of financing sought by early-stage companies seeking to grow rapidly.

VOLATILITY: The extent of fluctuation in share price, interest rates, and other factors relating to stock value. The higher the volatility, the less certain an investor is of return.

In order to achieve millionaire status, you must apply the principles. The key thing to remember is that becoming a millionaire is completely within your grasp if you follow all of the suggestions made in this book.

CONCLUSION

Congratulations! By now, you should feel good about your prospects for becoming a millionaire. *Simple Principles™ to Become a Millionaire* has helped you see where you must make changes in your life to articulate your goals, craft a plan, believe in yourself and your abilities, unlock your creative impulses, increase your earning potential, save money, learn to invest, and, most important, replace bad habits with new ones that are magnets to attract wealth.

If you have followed the hints, tips, tricks, ideas, suggestions, and other principles contained in this book, you are closer than ever to becoming a millionaire. Make sure to read every chapter in this book, even if you don't think it applies to you at first. Once you have gone through this book from beginning to end, you should have a good idea of how to apply the secrets of becoming a millionaire to your own life. The more than 200 principles included in this book have shown you that change is possible, and that becoming a millionaire is within your reach.

Reading this book is only the first step in that journey, however. As you move forward, you will need to know where to look for solutions, guidance, and advice when you are faced with a challenge. Therefore, think of this book as your constant companion for your journey toward wealth. Practice what you have learned in this book often. Keep it with you for easy reference. Consult it when you seek a specific solution. Refer to it when you need a reminder or want to be inspired. Think of the principles and exercises in *Simple Principles™ to Become a Millionaire* as roadmaps — they show you how to get from where you are now to where you want to be. In order to get there, you must apply the principles. The key thing to remember is that becoming a millionaire is completely within your grasp if you follow all the suggestions made in this book.

Tell Us Your Story

Simple Principles™ to Become a Millionaire has changed the lives of countless people, helping them make and save more money than they ever imagined. Now we want to hear your story about how this book has increased your wealth.

Tell us ...
- Why did you purchase this book?
- Which areas of your finances did you want to improve?
- How did this book help you improve in those areas?
- How did this book change your life?
- Which principles did you like the most?
- What did you like most about this book?
- Would you recommend this book to others?

Email us your response at info@wspublishinggroup.com or write to us at:

WS Publishing Group
7290 Navajo Road, Suite 207
San Diego, CA 92119

Please include your name and an email address and/or phone number where you can be reached.

Please let us know if WS Publishing may or may not use your story and/or name in future book titles, and if you would be interested in participating in radio or TV interviews.